Mobility for Special Needs

Juliet Stone

CASSELL

Cassell
Wellington House
125 Strand
London WC2R 0BB

215 Park Avenue South
New York
NY 10003

British Library Cataloguing-in-Publication Data
A catalogue record for this book is available from the British Library.

ISBN 0-304-33067-1 (hardback)
       0-304-33065-5 (paperback)

Typeset by Chapter One (London)
Printed and bound in Great Britain by Biddles Ltd, Guildford and King's Lynn

Contents

Acknowledgements

I gratefully acknowledge the children and young people who have taught me almost all I know and my colleagues, the mobility specialists who have taught me the rest.

I also thank Martyn, Ron, Shirley and Nick – they know the part they played.

Also to my son Steve for the diagrams.

Editorial foreword

This is much more than a book about mobility training for children with visual impairments. It is a book which has a great deal to say about supporting a wide range of children with special educational needs in everyday living, in their own homes, in their immediate neighbourhoods and communities, as well as in their local schools. While much of the detailed advice which it contains is focused on children with visual impairments, the book can profitably be read as a set of principles and guidelines which are relevant to supporting pupils with other impairments and disabilities and with a wide range of needs.

The book reflects a number of key themes which apply to all forms of support: the process of achieving greater independence and autonomy; the delicate nature of the changing relationship between the supporter and the person being supported; striking a balance between doing too much and too little; the influence of motivation on feelings of confidence and competence in achieving new goals.

At the same time, the book makes invaluable suggestions on how the environment can be changed in small and subtle ways to facilitate inclusion. We are also reminded about the importance of the attitudes of teachers and other colleagues to mobility teaching and indeed to other therapeutic interventions, reflected in comments which seem to view such interventions as an optional luxury and as irrelevant to the main work of the school.

Juliet Stone is to be congratulated on providing not only an authoritative guide to mobility training for pupils with a visual impairment but an important text for all professionals and parents concerned with supporting pupils with special needs in schools and in the community.

Professor Peter Mittler
Manchester
April 1995

Preface

Why a book on mobility and orientation? There are already several good books on the subject. Good as they are, the majority of the ones available in Great Britain emanate from the United States of America, where the education system is different, much of the environmental language is different (for example, sidewalks instead of pavements) and some of the mobility terminology varies from that used elsewhere.

In addition, the strong feeling of the writer and some others that other children with special educational needs, besides those with visual impairments, have a need for and a right to mobility and orientation education meant that a different approach might usefully add to the literature available. There is much research needed into the most appropriate programmes for children with special educational needs, particularly those with learning difficulties. It is hoped that this book will provoke others to further research in this area and to produce more useful material.

—1—

An overview of mobility and orientation

What do we mean when we talk about mobility and orientation? It is, quite simply, the ability to move around in our environment, travelling from one place to another in safety. This is a function which those of us without disabilities take for granted. When getting up in the morning we do not have to think about how to get to our kitchen. Nor, for the most part, do we have to think about how to get to the shops or how to get to work. While we are making these journeys, we do not spend the time thinking about how or where we are moving. This is quite apparent from the number of us who arrive at our destination wondering how we got there, having no recollection about the journey at all. Frequently, drivers are concerned that they have travelled several miles without, seemingly, thinking about it at all. We also know the feeling of having made a journey to find that we have arrived at the wrong place for that particular time or day, so automatic has our travel been. If we find that roads are blocked off and diversions are needed it is then that we have to make decisions about where we are going. It is, perhaps, only when we are hindered through our bodies in some way that we stop to think about moving around. For instance, people who suffer with bad backs know the feeling of looking at a flight of stairs and having to think about how moving up or down the stairs is going to be accomplished. Concerned about the pain of movement, they plan the best strategy, whether that is going up the stairs sideways or coming down on their bottoms.

Most of us have the ability to move around our environment safely, efficiently and independently. Our physical movements are automatic and our vision gives us immediate information about our environment and how we relate to it. These two aspects, the physical movement and the understanding of how we relate to the space around us, are both crucial in successful journey making. Mobility is the term which is usually given to physical movement and the negotiation of any obstacles and hazards. Orientation is the term used for the understanding of space and navigation within it. Any difficulty with either of these aspects is going to impede the ability to move independently.

It has been recognized for some years that children with little or no vision may have tremendous problems with their mobility and orientation. Research has been undertaken and, as a result, many techniques have been developed to help these children achieve independent travel. This book focuses on these strategies, the majority of the examples described referring to children with visual impairments. However, children with other disabilities and special needs may also find difficulty in these areas. Such children will be helped with programmes of intervention. The techniques used with the visually impaired can highlight the needs of other pupils and, in addition, many techniques and teaching strategies can be adapted to suit individual children.

Mobility

Mobility is the ability to move oneself without coming to any harm. Safe travel involves being able to avoid bumping into objects or tripping and falling over or off changes in walking levels. The traveller must be able to detect these hazards and take evasive action. In order to do this, travellers with visual impairments may use a long cane, a guide cane, a guide dog, or an electronic aid. Travellers with physical disabilities may use crutches, rollators or wheelchairs, and of course both groups will use the help of other people.

Orientation

Most children wanting to move from one place to another do so almost unconsciously. With very little mental effort, they decide how to move from where they are to where they want to be. They then have to take no further thought, they simply walk to their destination through the use of visual landmarks, at the same time observing obstacles which must be avoided. For people who have special needs, this decision-making and navigation may be a complicated process. In order to learn a route they must understand what changes of direction need to be made. In addition, they must learn to recognize landmarks which appear on the route. When these landmarks are identified, they must deduce from them where on the journey they are and take appropriate action. Negotiating a route may involve taking the responsibility of knowing where it is safe to cross a road and how to do so. This is particularly difficult for children with visual impairments but other children may also have difficulty. However, with very specific and long-term intervention these problems can be overcome.

Orientation involves having an awareness of space and an under-standing of the situation of the body within it. Good orientation means being able to answer the questions: where am I, where do I want to get to and how do I get there? (Hill and Blasch, 1980). For children who are visually impaired, particularly for those who have never seen, or for children who have learning difficulties, finding the answers to these questions may take several years. This is con-sidered further in the chapter on orientation.

WHY ARE MOBILITY AND ORIENTATION SO IMPORTANT?

It is easy to see why the skills of mobility and orientation are so important. The ability to move in and around the environment is critical and any inability to do so affects the individual psychologi-cally, socially, emotionally, economically and physically. Children and young people who have disabilities may have difficulties with their independent travel and the effect of these on their develop-ment and quality of life may be very considerable. Describing the effect of a visual impairment, Koestler (1976) said 'The loss of power to move about freely and safely is arguably the greatest deprivation inflicted by blindness'. The same may be felt by other people with disabilities which prevent or hinder independent travel.

Psychological aspects

There is a direct connection between movement and learning. It is through moving within our environment that an understanding of the world around us is developed. Children who are visually impaired are severely restricted in the variety and quantity of the concepts that they can experience (Lowenfeld, 1971). Children who have other physical disabilities may be restricted within certain boundaries. If they are unable to be mobile and move freely within their homes, schools or in any wider environment, their experiences will also be restricted. Although adults with the children can obvi-ously move them around, this dependence on another gives little opportunity for the children to follow their own inclinations in exploration. Without the ability to move freely, children's know-ledge of the world around them can become very second-hand, only perceived through what they are told and what they read. If chil-dren are able to move independently their world expands and they can be exposed to a far wider range of real experiences. This will feed into all their development and learning, including their language, literacy and understanding of concepts. Moving around independently involves problem-solving and risk-taking. Understanding danger, taking risks and accepting responsibility for these is an important part of personal development.

Social aspects

An important part of most people's social lives takes place outside the home; it is in the wider community that we make new social contacts. A large number of people do live alone and have little contact with people outside the home. This is particularly true for elderly people, whose walk to the post office for their pension or to the local shop may be their only social contact with other people. The ability to walk just two hundred yards or so can greatly add to the social interactions that can be enjoyed, and if this ability to travel independently can be extended, so also are the quantity and quality of social contacts that are possible. Visits to other people's homes, clubs, theatres and cinemas, sports venues, pubs, discos all become possible. The environment can be extended further if the use of public transport can be mastered.

Emotional aspects

If a person is unable to travel independently, this can have a devastating effect on their self-concept. Of course, it is possible to move around the environment with the help of other people, but this puts travellers with disabilities into a dependent situation. They are reliant on other people as to the frequency and timings of trips out and if this is not handled sensitively the help given can leave people feeling, and being seen as, helpless citizens. For the young person, taking part in social activities outside the home becomes an important part of social relationships and breaking free of the home and the parental environment necessitates being able to move in the community.

Physical aspects

Some teachers and mobility specialists say that they can identify a child or young person with a visual impairment, simply from their posture, the appearance of their feet and legs or the way they walk. A visual impairment is likely to impede free, relaxed and speedy movement and it is this type of movement which improves posture, develops leg and feet muscles and improves the walking gait. Any lack of movement prevents good physical development, and, in turn, any lack of good physical development will prevent good movement. This is true, not only of children who have visual impairments, but also of children with learning disabilities. Many children and young people are taken to school in a taxi and take little physical exercise, other than is arranged at school. For some pupils with special needs who are placed within mainstream schools, physical education becomes neglected. A lack of physical exercise can mean that children with special needs do not develop the flexibility and suppleness of their bodies, nor develop sufficient stamina to undertake mobility training. Frequently, mobility specialists comment that they need to initiate a programme to improve fitness levels in their pupils before they are able to undertake formal mobility training. I worked with one young woman of 15 who had a severe visual impairment. She was so unfit that she was unable to walk for a hundred yards without becoming out of breath. The mobility training was slow, not because she was incapable, but because we had to keep stopping for her to rest. Mobility education will be one way to get young people fit and the improved fitness will lead to an ability to undertake more intensive training.

Economic aspects

To be able to move independently within the environment is one of the pre-requisites for employment (Hill, 1986). It is true that there are occupations which can be undertaken at home. However, for the most part these are dull, repetitive jobs which are poorly paid. In addition, one of the most important needs for all of us is social interaction and again, for many of us, our employment is one of the main channels for this. In the past there was a tendency in educators of people with special needs, particularly the visually impaired, to see academic qualifications as a guaranteed route to employment. Frequently, the curriculum was geared to the pursuit of academic awards, to the exclusion of independent living skills. This meant, in many cases, that young people were leaving colleges and universities with a high level of qualification, but with an almost total lack of mobility skills, leaving them virtually unemployable. Even today there are people with special needs who find it difficult to get work, not because of their lack of ability, qualifications or training but because of difficulties in travelling to and from their places of work. Although for people with visual impairments a sighted guide may be a possibility for irregular and infrequent journeys, it is unlikely to be a solution for travelling to and from work.

Even for people who do not need to travel to and from their employment, an inability to travel independently can mean that any journey becomes a very expensive business. Taxis have to be used instead of trains or buses, and this may well limit the number of journeys outside the home that can be made.

WAYS IN WHICH A DISABILITY MAY AFFECT MOBILITY AND ORIENTATION

While mobility specialists working with visually impaired people have come to appreciate the many dimensions of travel problems, professionals working with persons having other primary limitations have not always recognized similar problems in their clients (Welsh, 1980). Unfortunately this is still true, although there are instances in schools and colleges for children and young people with special needs, where there are examples of programmes in orientation education. However, most professionals have not yet realized the importance of their expertise in developing these programmes for children and young people. Physiotherapists provide support and teaching in basic mobility for persons who have lost the full use of their legs or who have other neuromuscular problems, but this therapy is usually only provided within hospitals or schools. It does not cover all the requirements for travel in real life. For example, the activities do not generally cover orientation or strategies for moving around the outside environment. Children are rarely taught how to solicit assistance when needed or how to cope with the possible stigmatizing nature of their disability. Educators of children with hearing impairments may teach the client how to communicate in situations when aid is needed, but they do not usually provide experiences in real travel situations. Neither do they deal with the reactions of the children to dangers when they occur. Teachers of children with learning disabilities often teach their students to recognize bus and street signs and may take them on group trips. However, few of the programmes include helping them to become confident with strategies for coping with disorientation and other problems when travelling alone (Welsh, 1980). In the real environment there is a bombardment of stimuli and a variety of competing concerns over and above the reason for the journey, such as hazards, the reactions of passers-by, the possibility of getting lost. Children with disabilities may all find difficulties with travelling in the modern environment.

Children with a hearing impairment

For most children with a hearing impairment, even those with profound deafness, there will be no difficulties with mobility and orientation. The one exception to this may be problems with crossing the road, when hearing gives us important information. This information will not be available to children with severe hearing impairments, who should be taught, and encouraged to use, specific strategies when crossing roads. Their use of vision will be critical.

However, if there are other additional disabilities, even if these are minor in effect, there may be implications for the children's movement. This is discussed further in Chapter 7.

Children with learning difficulties

To travel safely within an environment we need the ability to process information received through the senses, interpret it correctly and to make decisions. The skill of independent travel requires a person to have a clear and functional understanding of areas, shapes and the constructs in the environment such as streets, road junctions and the layout of neighbourhood and buildings. For many children and young people with learning disabilities, these skills are difficult to master. They may have difficulties with analysing and synthesizing the information. They frequently have poorly developed motor co-ordination which results in a lack of understanding of their bodies and the way these work. In addition, many have perceptual problems. They may be confused when out of their normal routine or in strange or crowded places. This confusion will affect their decision-making processes, such as those required in making journeys. Another difficulty for these children and young people is their lack of problem-solving skills. They may be unable to re-orientate themselves if lost or to find an alternative route if one is blocked. Much of the information available in the environment to help people travel efficiently is given through the use of graphics. These are often difficult for children and young people with learning disabilities to understand, particularly with the vast differences in the systems of graphics used. Other information which aids travel is given through numbers. Examples of this are house and flat numbers, room numbers and those used on public transport. The concept of figures and numbering may be difficult, while certain perceptual problems may result in the children not being able to judge the depth of a step or distinguish other features in the environment. This can make the environment a terrifying place. All these difficulties can lead to a lack of confidence and this is sometimes exacerbated by the fact that some children are given little opportunity to be responsible for themselves.

Children with physical disabilities

It is obvious that a physical disability will affect a child's ability to move within the environment. As Hart says (1980), 'If one is oriented but not mobile, one cannot get to where one desires'. For children who are confined to wheelchairs and who are dependent on being pushed by an adult, even the experience of the environment will be different from that of children who are ambulant. The height at which one experiences movement will be constant – at the height of the wheelchair. Their experience of objects at low and high levels will be limited and some missed altogether. Distant objects may not be seen because buildings obscure them. The speed at which children are moved in the wheelchair is likely to be different from that of walking speed and incidental environmental factors may not be appreciated. The routes that are taken will depend on accessibility for the wheelchair and need not necessarily be the most direct or the most interesting. Children who spend a long time in a wheelchair will not have the same tactile experiences of different surfaces, such as those of walls and floors. However, children and young people with less severe physical disabilities may also require some support in achieving full independence. Poor posture and gait can make movement through the environment difficult, inefficient, or uncomfortable and may well impede the reactions and therefore the responses the children are able to make to danger.

Children who are blind

It is obvious that a visual impairment will affect the achievement of independent mobility. However, it may not be realized that the needs of those who are born with a visual impairment and those who become visually impaired later in life are different. The differences between the two groups are clearly demonstrated in the area of orientation. People who become blind later in life and who therefore have long experience of seeing and moving within the environment and of using maps and so on, will understand routes and be able to form mental concepts of the space around them. These people will know, for example, what a building is like, will understand how rooms fit together, what form staircases are likely to take and the fact that corridors will probably follow the same pattern on different floors. Adventitiously visually impaired people will have to adapt to using a mental mapping system, rather than a visual one, but their basic understanding of space and themselves within it is probably very good.

Children who are born with a visual impairment have very different experiences from the adventitiously visually impaired. They will never have seen space and, as a result, their mental map of the world and their own position in it may be very poor. They may have very considerable problems in forming correct concepts of their own bodies and then in understanding the space around them. In addition, many of these children experience a delay in all areas of their development (Tobin, 1979), all of which will affect their progress to independent travel. A survey carried out by the Royal

National Institute for the Blind in 1992 (Walker *et al.*) found that over 40 per cent of visually impaired children aged 12 years and over never go out alone. There is clearly some connection here with another fact the survey discovered, which is that only a quarter of visually impaired children have had any mobility training at all. The reasons for this are numerous and are discussed further in Chapter 8, but it is clear that some children's needs are not being met.

Children with low levels of vision

Until recently, mobility for those with low levels of vision had received little or no attention. The scarcity of trained mobility teachers in schools means, unfortunately, that in many cases this is still true. It is important that pupils with low vision should be assessed in their ability to travel independently. It is also essential that this assessment takes place in an unfamiliar environment. The way that youngsters move in and around an environment that they know well, such as their school, is no indicator of how they will function in a strange locality. Many of them will have reduced distance acuity or field loss which will seriously affect their ability to get around. Others may have difficulties with light or dark adaptation, which will mean that moving from indoors to outside or vice versa will be difficult, as they will take some time to adapt to the different lighting conditions. Pupils with photophobia, who seem to move around confidently on a cloudy day, may have extreme difficulty on a bright, sunny day. A route across a school campus when the sun is behind may be navigated easily. The reverse route facing the sun may leave the pupil nervous and confused. If distance vision is reduced, the use of certain landmarks, used by the fully sighted, may not be possible. Without clear vision, one's mental map needs to be more precise and one needs different and more frequent landmarks. Many pupils with a visual impairment have poor depth perception and may trip up on a kerb or perceive changes of depth which are not there, which is equally confusing.

Children whose condition causes double vision will also have difficulty getting about and will need specific training to cope with their faulty visual images. Other difficulties for the pupils with low vision may be identifying street names, house or bus numbers and destination signs. These could be seen as minor problems, but such difficulties can prevent children from being fully independent in their travel.

Pupils with eye conditions which cause night blindness, such as retinitis pigmentosa, need special consideration. Before their vision causes problems in school, they may well have been seriously restricted in their ability to get about in the evening or at night. Some of them may be unwilling to admit, even to themselves, that problems exist, preferring to make excuses for not going out in the evening. This can seriously affect their leisure and social activities. Pupils with conditions that might cause these difficulties should be assessed on their mobility in poor light. Although the mobility training for pupils with reduced vision will differ from that for pupils who are totally blind, the importance of such training cannot be denied.

MOBILITY AND ORIENTATION EDUCATION

Mobility and orientation programmes are usually referred to as skills training. This is probably an appropriate term for programmes with the adventitiously impaired, where a new set of skills is being incorporated into many years' experience of independent travel. However, for children who are born with disabilities, the term training does not seem appropriate. The programme of mobility and orientation education must be an integral part of such a child's total development and learning. It is not simply the learning of a set of skills that can be taught in a few weeks or months.

What is independence?

Earlier in this chapter, it was noted that a large number of children, aged 12 years and over and who have visual impairments, never go out alone. In the writer's experience this is also true of many children and young people with other disabilities. The aim of any mobility and orientation programme, therefore, is to increase the pupils' independence and in fact many young people achieve such a high standard of skill as a result of it that they are able to travel independently virtually anywhere. There is a tension between this ability and the fact that many parents of non-disabled children do not allow their children to travel anywhere alone. In the current climate, many parents feel unable to let their children face what seem to them to be unacceptable risks. However, in mobility programmes, young people with disabilities are being given the skills to travel independently and are encouraged to go out into an environment where they face these perceived dangers. Children and young people who have obvious physical, sensory or learning disabilities are demonstrably vulnerable. All children are taught not to speak to strangers, yet some of the children with visual impairments are given cards to show to the public stating that they require help. There is clearly no easy answer to these difficulties and a balance must be found between an over-protective attitude and the need to keep young people as safe as possible. This issue needs to be discussed fully by all those concerned and with the young people themselves. The term 'independence' clearly has a different meaning in different situations. When it is said that adults cross the street independently, it means that they can choose to go to any road junction and cross it. If it is said that an 11-year-old boy 'crosses the street independently', the interpretation is not quite as broad. The parents will exert some control over where he may go and when, but he will cross without necessarily having a helper nearby. When children are younger, they may be allowed to cross a quiet cul-de-sac street alone although there will be adults watching out for them. Each of these travellers will have reached an appropriate level of independence for their age.

Personality

There is no doubt that the personality of the people with a visual impairment greatly affects their attitude to travelling independently. A boy of 16, with whom I was working on his mobility education, described a visit to a large pop concert at Sheffield. Mark had been totally blind from birth. He had, however, an adventurous and out-going personality. Describing the journey to the sports stadium, Mark explained how he got separated from the two friends with whom he was travelling, about three-quarters of a mile from the venue. 'That threw me a bit', he said, 'because I hadn't really been taking much notice of where we were. But a group of other kids came along, I guessed they were going to the concert as well, so I just followed them.' 'What would have happened if they had just been going to the pub?', I asked. His quick retort was 'Well, I'd have been late for the concert'. 'Did you find your friends?' 'Yes, they were waiting at the gate for me.' He appeared to have found the whole experience great fun, including standing in the middle of a packed crowd for three hours while the concert was on. It will be readily appreciated why this young man took so easily to independent travel and why other young people, more shy and reserved, may find it more difficult. Many of the personality factors which make for successful mobility, such as assertiveness, a sense of humour and the ability to stay calm, can all be encouraged in the children. Developing these abilities is a cross-curriculum issue and would therefore involve other, or all, subject teachers.

Motivation

The most important factor in all children's learning is motivation and this is certainly true of mobility and orientation programmes. From the baby who moves to get to the toy that has gone out of reach, to the young person who wants to go to the town centre to buy the latest CD, it is having a reason to move that is important. Children with disabilities may not have this motivation. A blind baby who has lost a toy may not realize that by moving, the toy can be reached. The child with learning disabilities may not find anything to motivate her to move. It is the adults and other children who will need to provide the motivation. Unhappily, often the reverse happens. Young children can be discouraged from moving by parents and others who may bring toys to them rather than stimulating and supporting the children to move to the toys. Sometimes insufficient time and care is taken to discover what will motivate the individual child or young person to move. Occasionally, children and young people are actively discouraged from moving because of ignorance about the importance of this area. Unless children are motivated to move early in their lives, it may be very difficult to motivate them as they grow older, as they will have got too used to not having to move. Children who have been actively encouraged to move, explore, develop and satisfy their curiosity will have a willingness to face the challenges that will come later. A specialist or a manual is not necessarily needed to teach children with disabilities about the world. What is needed is for parents and others to get the children out of their homes and into the environment. No lesson plan is required for this. The children's curiosity will be the directing and guiding force. They will ask the questions; the parents will supply the answers as well as they can be answered for each child at the appropriate developmental level. The explanation should be accompanied whenever possible with 'hands-on' experience.

THE USE OF THE OTHER SENSES

Vision

It has already been noted that there are children and young people with low vision who require mobility and orientation input. One essential factor for these children will be to use their vision as effectively as possible. Children who are registered as blind may have residual vision which can be helpful in travel. Even being able to detect a light source, such as a line of windows in a corridor or a row of lights in a superstore, can be helpful in orientation. If children can detect colour this can be used to give additional information on routes. All children and young people with visual impairments should be assessed in terms of any low vision that might be useful.

Hearing

The use of the sense of hearing is very important in independent travel, particularly for children with a visual impairment. Children with physical disabilities may also have restrictions in the movement of their head and be unable to use their vision fully while travelling. It will be important for them also to use their sense of hearing. There are several stages in being able to use sounds effectively. In order to be able to make use of a sound, the children first have to discriminate it from other background sounds. The children must then be able to locate the sound as accurately as possible and identify the source. Finally, the children need to make decisions about their perceptions. Does the sound mean danger? Does it require avoiding action? Does the sound confirm that they are on the correct route? Children with learning difficulties may need help in achieving these various stages in using sound.

The kinaesthetic sense

This refers to the 'feel' of the body and its movements. We can feel whether our body is in a correct alignment, even when our eyes are closed. Our vision has helped us develop this sense by integrating what we feel with what we see of ourselves. The kinaesthetic sense tells us whether we are walking off balance, and allows us to detect errors of movement and correct them. It is the sense which gives information about what position our body is in and where our limbs are, when we have moved too fast or when we are about to fall off a chair. Children who have never seen may not have this sense well-developed.

The tactile sense

This sense is of great importance to children with visual impairments. They will need to have good tactual skills to determine what kind of walking surface they are on, for example grass as compared to paving. Their hands will be used to give them information about the environment and the objects within it. However, the sense of touch provides little or no information beyond that related to temperature, texture, and the shape of very small objects. Relationships such as size, distance and proportion, except where very small dimensions are involved, are perceived through the kinaesthetic sense functioning in conjunction with the sense of touch.

The understanding of the body

Poor body image and understanding of body concepts may cause problems. Directions such as 'turn left' or 'it's at waist height' will be meaningless unless the children have a basic understanding of the terms involved. It must be remembered that it is not only educationally blind children who have difficulty with such terms. Similarly, the ability to walk in a straight line, or to make accurate turns, so important in mobility, may not be developed in low-vision youngsters.

Attitudes

As has already been noted in the section on motivation, the attitude of those involved with children and young people is critical in the development of independence. Many parents, carers and teachers can develop an over-protective attitude, which although understandable will not allow the children to extend themselves and develop satisfactorily. High but realistic expectations can lead to some surprising achievements. 'I would never have believed he could ever do it' said a father about his 14-year-old son with severe learning difficulties. The boy had just made his first bus journey. The attitude of the general public will affect how well children and young people are able to travel within the community. As with the close family, people can vary from giving too much or inappropriate help to offering none at all, when what is needed is an awareness of the possible needs of travellers and an ability and willingness to help, after consultation with the travellers themselves. The following comment, made as long ago as the eighteenth century, refers to children who are visually impaired. It also, of course, applies to any child who has a disability.

> Parents and relations ought never to be too ready in offering their assistance to the blind in any office which they can perform, or in any acquisition which they can procure for themselves, whether they are prompted by amusement or necessity. Let a blind boy be permitted to walk through the neighbourhood without a guide, not only though he should run some hazard, but even though he should suffer some pain. From the time that he can move and feel let him be taught to supply his own exigencies, to dress and feed himself, to run from place to place either for exercise or in pursuit of his own toys or necessaries. In these excursions, however, it will be highly proper for the parent or tutor to superintend his motions at a distance, without seeming to watch over him.
>
> (Blacklock, eighteenth century, reported in Webster, 1980)

The rest of this chapter is mainly concerned with the strategies and aids which have been developed to help the visually impaired. The underlying principles can, however, also be applied to children with other special needs.

AIDS TO MOBILITY AND ORIENTATION FOR VISUALLY IMPAIRED PEOPLE

Guide dogs

Perhaps the aid most easily recognized by the general public is the guide dog. Surprisingly, only 2 per cent of the visually impaired population use guide dogs. The reasons for this are various and discussed later in this section.

The history of the development of using dogs as mobility aids for blind people is described in Chapter 8. There are, of course, many advantages in using a guide dog. The training that the dogs are given means that they are able to detect obstacles and drops in walking surfaces, such as pavement kerbs. Before the dog meets its owner, it has already been trained to a high standard. This is followed by a period of training for the owner with the dog. The dog's role is to help with the mobility side of moving in the environment, that is, avoiding obstacles on the walking surface and detecting 'drops' such as pavement kerbs. The most highly trained dogs can also detect obstacles at head height, such as overhanging branches. In addition, because the dog is taking care of the mobility side of travel, it leaves the owner free to concentrate on orientation. In addition, many guide dog owners would agree with the feelings of one young man who said 'Having a guide dog is a great way to attract the girls!' and the social side of using a guide dog is extremely important. Few of us can resist the appeal of guide dogs and they certainly facilitate social interactions.

There are, however, some disadvantages. First, dogs are not provided for children and young people under 16 years of age. Second, they can be inconvenient and they certainly are not collapsible. Third, there is also the walking speed to consider. Guide dogs prefer to walk at a speed of three to four miles an hour, which is faster than is comfortable for many people with visual impairments. (It must be remembered that the vast majority of people with visual impairments are over 70 years of age.) Fourth, guide dogs need care and attention and an opportunity for exercise, which many people are not able to provide. The use of a guide dog still requires the traveller to have good orientation skills. Guide dogs cannot find their way from one place to another. This perhaps seems obvious to some, but many members of the general public assume that guide dogs provide the orientation for the traveller and cite the dog who 'takes' the blind person from home to the shops or pub. If a particular route is made many times, the dog will certainly learn it, in the same way that many dogs know the regular routes of their owners. However, dogs do not know how to navigate and this has to be the responsibility of the owner. Finally, owning a guide dog does require a liking for dogs and, as is true with the rest of the population, not all people with a visual impairment have a fondness for the canine world.

The use of canes

There are a number of different canes which are used by the visually impaired population in this country. One of these is a symbol cane and is used as a means of identification only. It is not meant as a support. The symbol cane is useful for those who do not need formal mobility training, as the use of it will allow other pedestrians and drivers to recognize that assistance may be required. If the cane has red stripes on it, this signifies the user has both a hearing and a visual loss. Perhaps the most recognizable is the one known as the long cane, which is used to detect kerbs. The long cane is made of aluminium, with a crook at the top and a nylon tip at the bottom. Just below the crook is a rubber grip. The main aims for the design of the cane are that it should be 'rigid, durable, conductive, lightweight and inexpensive' (Hill, 1986). In terms of the last two requirements, long canes usually weigh between eight and ten ounces and in Britain the cost averages around £7. The length of the cane will vary with each person, according to the user's height. The cane is usually long enough to reach to the traveller's armpit. Other factors which determine the length of the cane are the speed of walking, the length of stride and the reaction time of the traveller. There are a variety of tips that can be put on the cane, including the fairly new rollating tip which rolls along the walking surface as the cane is used, which some travellers find easier to use.

The use of the long cane in mobility is described in Chapter 4 and the history of the development of the cane in mobility training is described in Chapter 8. There are several advantages to using a long cane. It gives advance information on the walking surface which allows the traveller time to stop before obstacles, kerbs or stairs. The cane is easily manoeuvrable. It is also, as has been noted above, inexpensive. There are canes which are collapsible, which means they can be folded up and put in the traveller's pocket when they are not being used. An additional advantage of the cane is that it identifies the user as visually impaired. This allows, or should allow, the general public to take avoiding action and also to offer help when appropriate.

There are also some disadvantages which need stating. While the long cane certainly gives information on the walking surface, it does leave the upper body unprotected, and travellers using the cane get no information about overhanging bushes or trees. Walking into these can be frightening. In addition, as has been noted, the cane identifies the user as visually impaired and the advantages of this have already been described. However, many people, especially those in adolescence or young adulthood, do not wish to be identified. Many teachers of mobility have shared the writer's experience of introducing the cane to one young man, and receiving the comment 'Use one of those – you must be joking! My mates will think I'm mad.' There is a more simple cane which is similar in shape, but is not so sturdy. This is known as the guide cane and is used by travellers who only need to use it occasionally, for instance for detecting kerbs.

Electronic aids

A number of different electronic aids have been devised over the past 20 years. Farmer (1980) describes an electronic aid as 'a device that sends out signals to sense the environment within a certain range or distance, processes the information received and furnishes the user with certain relevant bits of information about the environment'. One example of an electronic aid is the sonic guide.

This aid is mounted into spectacle frames and the user also carries a power pack. It uses sonar waves which are transmitted to the immediate environment and then received back. The sonar waves are then translated into auditory signals which can be understood by the user. The aim of the aids is to enable the user to detect the distance and direction of objects and also discriminate between the different surfaces of objects. In the 1970s there were several research studies into the use of the sonic aid. One of these was done by Bower (1977). He used the aid with very young children to help them with the exploration of space. Bower felt that the aid had great possibilities, but the use of it was not extended to many children, as Bower's enthusiasm was not shared by other professionals. The advantage of an electronic aid is that it detects objects and, through the pitch or loudness of sound, gives the user an estimate of how far away the object is. However, at present, the majority of these types of aid are expensive and they are also fairly fragile.

A recent electronic aid which is beginning to be used more widely in Britain is the Walkmate Sonic Pathfinder. This is worn in the same manner as personal radios and cassette players. It has a small compact pack which can be clipped on the belt, and has earphones attached to it. The Pathfinder detects objects and the information is given either through vibrations or by sound. The main advantage of this aid is that it is unobtrusive and young people particularly find this important. It is also efficient and inexpensive, costing about £200. One young man, who had recently lost his sight and who found it difficult to develop the use of his other senses, found that the Pathfinder solved many of his problems. However, any aid must be chosen after consideration of the strengths and difficulties of the individual.

SIGHTED GUIDE

Although one of the aims of a mobility and orientation programme is independence, the help of other people will be needed in many situations. This can be a carer carrying the young child around, a person pushing the wheelchair, or a sighted person guiding a visually impaired person. The problems for children in wheelchairs are dealt with more fully in Chapter 6; however, the general principles of assisting any child with a special need are the same. If efficiently done, the use of a sighted guide can be a very safe method of travel. In addition, the guide can give information on the environment which aids the traveller's understanding of space and orientation within it and also adds to the enjoyment of travel. Yet another advantage of human guiding is that it guarantees social contact and the importance of this should not be underestimated.

The relationship between the guide and the traveller is crucial and is based on trust. It is critically important that the person guiding knows what she or he is doing and feels confident. Many visually impaired and physically disabled people have stories to tell of incidents that have happened to them, including the wheelchair user who was tipped up off the kerb into the road by the person pushing the wheelchair! A blind friend of mine had developed, over many years, complete confidence in my ability to guide her. One day, we were chatting away while walking through a city centre and I allowed her to walk into a lamp post. This was sheer carelessness on my part. While she still, amazingly, allows me to guide her, she admits that her trust in me is now marred and that part of her is now very wary of what might happen. I, too, am aware that her grip on my arm is not as relaxed as it used to be. The technique for being a sighted guide is described at the end of this chapter. However, it needs to be said here that the guide must concentrate on the guiding. We are used to protecting our own walking space, doing so automatically. It is a very different thing to be aware of the space to one side of us, both the ground surface, such as any obstacles or any changes in level, and the space above, such as overhanging trees, or road signs. It takes a conscious effort to do so.

Another disadvantage is the fact that most of the general public do not know how to be of use to a traveller with a disability and can often be more of a hindrance than a help. A further difficulty with relying on the help of other people is that travel depends on the human guide being there, which may not necessarily always be possible. Perhaps the greatest disadvantage is that using a guide does foster dependence on other people, and this can adversely affect both the traveller's own self-esteem and the views of other people. These effects can be lessened if the correct techniques are used, as these give some of the responsibility to the traveller, enabling him or her to use the guide as simply an aid to travel.

General principles of guiding include the following:

1 Do not manhandle!
2 Stay in front of the person, never push from behind.
3 Adjust walking speed to suit the guided person and watch for fatigue. Being guided can be a tiring business.
4 Do not leave visually impaired people in an open space. Always leave them in contact with furniture or a wall.
5 As you travel, give information that not only adds to the interest of the journey, but also helps to establish orientation to an area.
6 Pay attention to where you are both going. Be aware of the other person's walking surface and any overhead obstacles.
7 Practise guiding skills. If you are not sure of what you are doing, your lack of confidence will transmit itself to the visually impaired person. Furthermore, if guiding is done efficiently, it becomes unobtrusive and gives dignity to the guided person.

There are some specific techniques that are helpful to use when guiding visually impaired people.

The basic technique

The traveller holds the guide's arm a little above the elbow with the thumb on the outside and the fingers curled round the inside. To give maximum control, both guide and guided should keep the upper arms held closely to the body. The traveller should remain half a step behind the guide, thus protected by the guide's body (Figure 1.1). It can sometimes be appropriate for the two people to link arms but the guide must then take extra care to look out for the wider space at the side of them (Figure 1.2).

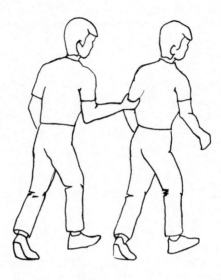

Figure 1.1

When walking, the visually impaired person must always feel in control. The speed of the guide can be altered by either pulling back gently on the arm or nudging it forward. This is important as it can be as difficult and stressful to walk too slowly as to move too quickly.

Figure 1.2

Negotiating doors can often cause problems and there is often a tendency for the guide to push the traveller through the door. To enable the traveller to have control of the door and therefore to feel less afraid that the door will trap him or her, the guide must approach the door on the hinge side. This may mean changing sides with the guide, but this is easily done. The traveller simply holds the guide's arm with the other hand and then trails the free hand across the guide's back and takes the other arm. Once the door is reached, the guide takes hold of the handle, which will indicate the position of it to the traveller (Figure 1.3). The latter then takes hold of it with the free hand. The traveller can then pull or push the door open, and move through the doorway, closing the door when it is sensible to do so.

Figure 1.3

Moving up and down flights of stairs can be a stressful situation for the visually impaired person, especially going down. Although verbal information will be helpful, the traveller will detect the direction up or down through the movement of the guide's body. When the stairs are reached, the guide moves on to the first step and pauses. The traveller can feel from the movement whether the steps go up or down (Figure 1.4).

When the traveller is ready to proceed, she or he can nudge the guide's arm and the ascent or descent can be continued. When the end of the flight is reached, the levelling off of the guide's body

Figure 1.4

should be felt by the traveller. But here again, verbal help or a slight pause can be helpful.

When guiding a visually impaired person to a seat or chair, the back of the chair should always be shown so that the traveller can seat him or herself, the guide having ensured that the seat is free of cats, books and so on! There are other techniques, such as for getting in and out of cars, which should be taught to people with visual impairments. The list of additional reading at the back of this book includes examples of these.

The key words for all these skills are control and dignity. Having to be dependent on a sighted guide can be a difficult, even humiliating, experience. Giving control to the traveller can do much to minimize this.

Guiding the child

Guiding young children is slightly different from guiding another adult. This is mainly because of the differences in height between the adult guide and the child. The technique described above can be modified to make it suitable for this situation. Instead of holding the guide's arm, the child can hold the adult's wrist; this is usually found to be appropriate, and looks very natural. If the children are very young or do not fully understand what is meant by guiding, it may be necessary for the adult to hold the child's hand. As soon as possible, however, children should learn to hold, rather than be held. This transfers some of the responsibility to the child, which is important and will also enable a smooth transfer to the adult guiding technique.

However, whichever modified grip is used, adults do need to remember that the walking space they have to oversee is larger than when walking with an adult who will be walking slightly behind them. It is surprisingly difficult to watch out for another person's walking surface. We are so used to looking out for the space immediately in front of us that to pay attention to the walking surface several feet to the side of us as well takes a great deal of concentration. It is important that children develop a trust in their guides, and every effort must be made to ensure that no unforeseen mishap occurs. Children who have found that their trust is misplaced take a long time to develop it again, and may become fearful of making any movement.

This chapter has given an overview of the numerous aspects of mobility and orientation. Successive chapters deal with many of these in more detail.

—2—
The young child

INTRODUCTION

Anyone who has been involved with young children will know the love of movement which they demonstrate. Young children enjoy practising and extending their physical skills. They will climb up anything that's climbable and spend their time hopping, skipping, galloping, going in, over and under obstacles. This is vital, not only for the development of their bodies, but also for the development of their movement and spatial concepts. By going in, through, under and over, they learn the meaning of these words and learn how objects in space are related to each other and how they can be negotiated.

As well as extending the actual mastery of skills, young children need to develop their stamina and strength. Fortunately, they love to do so. Once they can walk, they want to walk all the time, however tired they are. When the more sophisticated skill of running has been mastered, they hardly ever want to keep still. Many a parent has expressed a wish for the same amount of energy which their children exhibit! If we present children with a hill they will run up it, slide down and begin again. Perhaps some of us adults have lost the love of extending our physical prowess, and the thorough enjoyment of feeling really breathless and physically tired, but children love it. For some children with disabilities, these experiences may not be possible and they may never learn to love movement or have the opportunity to extend their physical abilities.

PARENTS AND CARERS

Before considering how parents and carers can encourage good physical development in their children with disabilities, it is important to remember the effect the birth of a baby with a disability may have on the parents and the rest of the family. The parents are going to be the most important people in the baby's life and their involvement in the baby's development will be crucial. As the parents' involvement in any programme of intervention is so necessary, some of the important parts of their role are described here.

As every child is an individual, whether he or she has special needs or not, so too is the family and its culture. This individuality must be taken into account by everyone involved. The reaction to the birth of a baby will be individual and although the literature suggests the different stages of reaction that families may experience, the timing of these stages and indeed the stages themselves will vary from family to family (Stone, 1993). Some families will develop a very protective attitude. This will affect the way they view allowing their toddler to climb stairs, play outside or even move at all. One family, for the best of reasons, kept their blind baby girl within the confines of a playpen for most of the day. Opportunities to move and explore the environment were very restricted. This child became so fearful of moving that it was some years before she would walk by herself. In other families it is not the parents who are wanting to over-protect the young child, but the extended family, the grandparents, aunts and uncles. The pressure on the parents from relations and neighbours can be hard to resist, whatever their own feelings may be.

Some families take a very different view, and expect their child to behave in the same way as children without disabilities. They may expose their child to a frightening world before the child has any strategies to deal with it. It is right, of course, to challenge children and allow them the feeling of achievement in overcoming challenges, but this can be taken to an extreme. As a result a child may become too fearful to move at all. Most families, of course, come somewhere between these two extremes and are sometimes confused when trying to find the balance between keeping their child safe and allowing them the freedom to move. Any professional who works with a family needs to understand and respect these differences in attitudes and feelings. Individual programmes for the child will also have to take into account these differences.

It is also important to realize that however involved parents may wish to be with the education of their child, the pressures on their time and levels of energy may be great. The pressures of work, other children and family problems may leave parents little time or energy to devote to a programme of activities with their disabled child. Fortunately, many intervention strategies to develop the early movement of their child can be incorporated into daily routine and activities.

As children with sensory and learning disabilities are likely to follow the same progression of development as other children, it is useful to note some of the critical stages.

EARLY PHYSICAL DEVELOPMENT

Kephart *et al.* (1974) state that the motor system is the initial system in the hierarchy of development. The development of motor skills gives an impetus to the development of children's cognitive skills. Individual children of course develop at different rates, but the milestones in the physical development of young children follow the same progression. The impact of a disability can then be appreciated and intervention strategies can be devised which will be appropriate for the particular stage of development.

Babies first develop control over their heads and some babies of a few days old can hold their heads up for a few minutes. At 7 months, when lying on the floor, they are able to roll over from their backs on to their tummies and back again. Soon after this they start crawling. By 8 months they are able to sit momentarily, without any external support, and most babies are pulling themselves to a standing position and walking while holding on to furniture soon after 1 year of age. Independent walking is usually achieved by 15 months (Bower, 1977).

The protective reflexes also develop in certain stages. At 6 months a baby can protect itself if it falls forward, but is unable to do so if it falls backwards. By 8 months, a baby is able to protect itself if it falls sideways. Many of us will have enjoyed watching an infant test these reflexes by leaning from side to side and putting its hand out at the last second to stop the fall. At the age of 1 year, most babies can protect themselves in all directions. These reflexes are clearly very important in the development of the motor system and in the infants' feeling of control over their bodies.

Children need practice at each stage to be developmentally ready for the next. For example, when children first stand, they do so momentarily and then, gradually, can do it for longer periods. This in itself helps develop the balancing skills necessary for walking. At this stage, too, children are developing and refining the crucial protective reactions for walking and they also develop the necessary hip rotation for walking. Efficient and effective walking demands not only the removal of bad posture and gait in the walking movement. It also requires the 'development of righting actions, balance, protective reactions, rotation and normal muscle tone' (Farmer, 1980). Without these abilities the child will be unable to refine walking skills and move on to more complex movements such as running and jumping.

As children grow and continue to expand the range and extent of physical movement, the aspects of agility, flexibility, stamina, strength and relaxation of muscles are developed. These skills are needed throughout life and the basis for future movement is set in the early physical activities of young children.

Children with disabilities

The physical development of children with special needs may be different from that of an ordinary child. This may be the direct result of the child's particular disability, as in the case of a child with cerebral palsy. Clearly the development of motor skills will be different for this child from that of a child without a physical disability. However, indirect influences of a disability may also interfere with development. A child with a visual impairment has the same potential for physical development as a fully sighted child. The effects of the visual impairment, however, will mean that the motivation to move will be reduced and the fear of moving will be increased. These two factors may prevent the child having the necessary experience to develop physically at the same time as the sighted child. It will be important to understand the differences between these direct and indirect influences of the disability and to devise intervention strategies for both.

Sonsken *et al.* (1984) discussed the implications of a visual impairment on the physical and motor development of babies. They listed seven ways in which the development could be affected, including diminished drive (or lack of motivation), poor body image, reduced opportunity, delayed concept development and sensory-motor integration, and fear. Sonsken's article is an important one for those interested in the early development of motor skills in young children with visual impairments and other special needs.

For children with special needs, particularly those with a visual impairment, the development of their body and spatial concepts may be difficult.

If we consider the experiences of blind and of sighted babies in the first few weeks and months, the impact of a severe visual impairment becomes clear. The sighted babies are bombarded by visual stimuli. These stimuli include light, colour, the horizontal and vertical, and movement. In addition, sighted babies soon see that the space around them has boundaries, ceilings, walls and so on. Babies with a visual impairment receive none of this information. They do not see the arrangement of the furniture in their room, nor the ceiling; they do not see the four walls of the room; nor can they see what objects are positioned along those walls. As they move their body position, they do not see the objects in the room change their position in relation to them, the fact that the cupboard door that was in front of them is now on their left as they move to the right.

Sighted babies learn quickly that there are sounds which come from objects and people. It may take several months for babies with a severe visual impairment to establish this concept. The stimuli these babies receive are very limited. Sounds come and go, but have no real relevance as the babies have no knowledge of what made them and whether these sources of sound are still present. In fact, the only reality to these babies is what they feel in terms of their bodies, in particular their hands. Their little fingers are very insensitive and although they may touch the breast, or the bottle, the information received is very fragmentary and gives little idea of the reality of what is being felt. These differences in the quality and quantity of experience (Lowenfeld, 1971) are likely to increase over the first few months.

Babies with physical disabilities will have different problems. Their body awareness may be very limited and if the babies are unable to control their head movements they may be unable to obtain the visual information about their environment. Their restricted movements may result in a lack of opportunity for free exploration and their understanding of the environment may be limited.

It is probable that children with disabilities will miss out on the very necessary activities for practising and extending the physical skills. For example, if they do not see well, or at all, the experience of running will be fraught with difficulties. They will be unable to launch themselves into space or move without constraint if they have to peer closely before taking every step. Children with learning difficulties may lack the motor co-ordination to run and in addition may have a disinclination to move generally. Fatigue or discomfort will deter the children with physical difficulties from moving. The implication for all these children is a possible lack of the development of stamina and muscle strength. Many children with special needs have poor posture, underdeveloped muscles and little stamina and, far from enjoying movement, will do all they can to avoid it.

However, there are many ways in which babies with special needs can be encouraged to develop an awareness of their bodies, many of which can be incorporated into the daily routine of the babies and young children.

Strategies for encouraging body awareness

Even in the earliest weeks and months, parents and carers can help the babies to develop an awareness of their bodies. For example, a very simple way is to tie a small bell to a ribbon and tie it round one of the ankles. This can be alternated between the two feet and then a bell can be put on each ankle. In some communities, this is a usual thing to do with all babies. Many babies wear Babygro or similar suits. Velcro can be used to attach interesting 'feels' or 'sounds' on the suits. (For safety reasons, this should be done only when a parent or carer is with the baby.) The babies will find these unintentionally at first, but will gradually be attracted to the sounds. In this way they will touch different parts of their bodies. This will help babies with disabilities begin to understand about their body parts and how they move and where they as individuals stop and the rest of the world begins. The daily routines of dressing and undressing can be used to introduce the babies to the interesting bits of their bodies, such as the individual fingers and toes, the back of the legs and so on. In addition, parents can tickle their babies, blow on their bodies, splash water around them in the bath and give them pleasurable experiences of their bodies. In this way, parents will be helping their children to establish a real understanding of their bodies and the way they move. Another way of developing the body concepts of young children is through lap games, such as 'Pat-a-cake', 'This little piggy went to market' or 'Bouncing to town'. Some young children with special needs may show discomfort or displeasure at being handled and moved. They may be frightened by movement and feel that there is safety in stillness. Firm but kindly handling will probably overcome the babies' dislike. If this reaction is very severe, advice from a therapist may be needed.

Parents of young children with special needs may find the input from a physiotherapist very helpful. This is probably understood when the needs of children with physical disabilities are being considered, but the in-depth knowledge of movement patterns which physiotherapists have, and their techniques for handling and moving very young children, can be invaluable for children with other special needs. In addition, parents can be advised on these techniques and shown how to encourage their babies to develop head control, to roll over, to develop muscle tone and the saving reflexes mentioned earlier. Parents should ask for help from a paediatric physiotherapist, as it may not be generally recognized the part these professionals have to play and their expertise may not be provided automatically.

As the children develop, they will need to understand other people's bodies in relation to theirs. Children with severe visual impairments and those with learning difficulties often find it difficult to grasp the concept of left and right on someone else. For example, when they are sitting on mother's lap and facing her, the mother's left arm will be in a different location to their own left arm. When they are standing side by side, the child's left side will be next to the mother's right side.

The first moves

Some babies with special needs may be delayed in crawling, standing and walking. Medical advice will be available for carers of
babies with physical disabilities. This advice will include which
movements to encourage in the babies and how to do so. Babies
with learning disabilities or with visual impairments can also be
encouraged to move and to crawl. Encouraging head control is
important. This can be done through laying the babies on their tummies on the floor for short periods. An adult or another child can
motivate the little ones to hold up their heads through the use of
their voices, or a noisy or bright toy. Some babies will not like being
on their tummies, but it is worth persevering as it is one of the
stages towards crawling. It is not, however, until the children learn
that they can reach for and grasp an object that they have any reason
to crawl. Reaching is the forerunner to creeping. Although babies
with severe visual impairments and some of those with learning difficulties may be physically ready to creep and have the ability to
support themselves on their hands and knees, some time may
elapse before they actually do so. Once the babies associate a sound
with an object, reach for and grasp it, then they are ready to crawl.
This is a particularly critical stage for babies with visual impairments as it is not until they are crawling or walking that they begin
to develop spatial awareness. They are unable to project their mental constructs beyond their reach. The children's crawling can be
encouraged through directing them through the movements, that is,
the left hand and right knee moving together, then the opposite
limbs.

   Some children do not crawl, but go straight from sitting to standing, and by not crawling they miss out a useful stage of development. Crawling helps to develop the muscles and it also gives the
opportunity to move while still remaining in contact with the floor,
which can give a feeling of security. During crawling, the head is in
the leading position and this may make the babies with visual
impairments feel vulnerable.

Standing and walking

Many children with special educational needs, particularly those
with visual impairments, use a very broad base for standing. They
stand with their feet well apart as this helps give them a feeling of
security and safety. As they start to walk, the use of this broad base
continues and they often walk in a very stiff-legged and flat-footed
way. This can develop into an unbalanced manner of walking.
To develop more refined and sophisticated skills, children need

continual feedback on their movement. This feedback is prevented or restricted by a physical disability, a learning difficulty or visual impairment. Children with physical disabilities may have impaired sensations of their own bodies and may not feel the difference between one posture or movement and another. Children with learning difficulties may not understand the difference between an efficient and an inefficient movement. For children with visual impairment, it is the lack of visual feedback that may restrict the development of fluent movement and it must be remembered that children with visual impairments cannot imitate the movements of others. Much of our learning about posture comes through our vision. Many readers will have had the experience of seeing their reflection in a shop window and immediately correcting their posture. Adults working with these children will need to explain and encourage correct posture. Children with learning disabilities may need similar help. They may not understand how to translate the posture and gait of other people into the way they themselves move and walk.

One way of helping children to understand the normal manner of walking is to stand the child on the adult's feet, with both child and adult facing the same way. The child will feel the adult's knees bend and the adult can also nudge the backs of the child's knees to encourage a relaxed movement. The posture and gait of the child may be tense and awkward. This may continue long after the child has gained confidence in walking because of the fear of moving into the unknown. Relaxation should be encouraged in any way possible and provided through other physical activities. After the children learn to walk, expect them to walk by themselves most of the time. They can learn their way around the house, garden and other homes which are visited regularly.

Some carers will be concerned about very young children with disabilities attempting to climb up and down stairs, but if they are physically able to, they should be encouraged to do so. Obviously the carer will stay very close to the child at the beginning of the encounter and may be able to provide guidance on the best way to negotiate the stairs. When carers are not able to watch the child, they may prefer to put up a stair-guard, but the child should be allowed to explore the stairs as frequently as possible. They will soon become confident and enjoy going up and down.

One important thing to remember is that all young children fall and trip over when they are learning to walk, run and so on. Children with special needs may have more falls than their non-disabled peers. While we will do all we can to keep them from harm, 'bumps and bruises' are to be expected and we can help them most by supporting them kindly through these falls, rather than preventing them from happening. They are going to need determination and courage as they grow older and these characteristics need developing early.

THE ENVIRONMENT

The environment is considered in more detail in Chapter 7. For the young child, a balance must be found between having an environment which is totally ordered and having one of total chaos. A mixture of the two is usually found in most homes. Children with visual impairments will find it helpful if the furniture is always in approximately the same place. Any critical changes to the arrangement of the furniture will need to be shown to them. Pathways and areas of the floor surface should be kept relatively clear of objects, so that the children can feel confident in moving. Nevertheless, it is good for them to realize that their younger brother or sister may have left some bricks or toy cars in their path. The youngsters need to be ready for the unexpected which they are certain to meet once they go into the wider environment.

Best (1992) describes some examples of minor adaptations to the home which can be useful for children with special needs, particularly those with visual and additional disabilities. He writes:

> Banisters are an example. They are most helpful if they are continuous and finish at least level with the bottom step so that the end of the banisters clearly indicates the end of the steps. Door handles, dado rails, table surfaces, wall coverings and so on can all be used to help establish position and direction of movement. Hand clues can also be introduced into a setting to provide extra support for a child. Plastic or wooden shapes can be fastened on to a child's chair, drawer and peg to make them easier to find; textured wallpaper can be added to a wall just in front of a door or near the beginning of a flight of stairs; distinctive handles can be used to help in the identification of different doors in a corridor. These extra clues need not necessarily draw attention to the blind child's special needs. For example, warning of a door in a corridor could be given by gluing several strands of nylon fishing line to the wall to form a tactile patch of vertical stripes. It will be easily felt by the child but go unnoticed by many sighted people.

For children who have physical disabilities, a more adapted environment may be necessary. Advice should be sought as to how to give the children as much access to the different places within the home as possible.

Extending the range of movement

The various aspects of physical development which need attention include stamina, suppleness, relaxation, posture, gait, co-ordination and total body control. These are learnt through the practice of the various new motor skills and through the opportunity for children to extend themselves physically. There can be a tendency to ignore this area of children's physical development. Once they are walking it may be assumed that children will acquire other movements incidentally. There may be a temptation to start to emphasize the children's need for fine motor skills which lead on to print writing or Braille reading. This can lead to adults focusing on 'table top' activities. However, the development of gross motor skills will always come before the fine motor skills. Children gain control over their limbs before the hands and fingers. It is through and because of the mastery of the gross motor that children can progress to the fine motor activities. It is also important to remember that there is an age appropriateness of the physical activities for a young child. It is far more appropriate and much easier to teach young children to skip, gallop, do 'head over heels', than to teach a teenager. These are not activities which a fully sighted teenager does and children need to take part in these activities when they are young. It is very difficult to motivate the older child who has never moved freely to do so. They have passed the age when it is a natural activity to develop these skills. It is necessary, wherever possible, to follow the normal developmental patterns of children. Success is more likely that way.

When appropriate for the individual child's physical condition, the typical rough and tumble of parent and child activities increases the child's body awareness, develops their saving reflexes and increases their understanding of space. When the children are dancing, moving to music or playing actively, they can be encouraged to stretch up high and outwards, roll in a ball, fold in half, and so on. Other marvellous opportunities are provided in soft play rooms, found in most special schools. These rooms consist of very large soft cushions which come in different shapes. They can be arranged to make slopes for the children to climb up and slide down. There are cushions which can provide a jumping platform and the whole environment is one where the children will feel safe and have no fear of hurting themselves. Outside, the children can roll down grassy slopes, swing on swings, play with large rubber tyres, jump on trampolines, attempt to use stilts and so on. The possibilities are endless.

Running is important as it develops children's stamina and strength. The writer recalls two 4-year-old blind children whom she took for a run. Holding hands, the three of them ran some fair distance across a field. Afterwards, one of the children said 'I've never done that before. Can we do it again?' and the other said 'Is this how Superman flies?'. These experiences are important for the children. To encourage and enable children with severe visual impairments to run, guide ropes can be provided. For example, a rope can be placed around the garden. The children can either hold on to the rope, or to prevent chafing to the hands they can hold on to a small hoop which is put on to the rope. They can, of course, hold an adult's hand and the running may do both of them good!

Water can be another helpful environment for many children with all types of disability. Activities in water and eventually swimming can develop all the physical aspects of development. Many swimming pools offer parent and toddler sessions and the children will soon become accustomed to the water if they begin experiencing it when they are young.

Extending the range of the children's movements will develop the mobility aspect of independent travel. Experiencing the environment will begin to develop their orientation skills.

Experiencing the environment

As children learn to crawl and walk they will be able to move around their homes, and if they are given the opportunity to explore they will soon learn the home environment. Children with severe visual impairments will use sound clues to orientate themselves. The sounds of the kettle or washing machine will tell them that they are in the kitchen. The noise of the clock or radio will tell them they are in the sitting room. It is helpful if there is not continual background noise as this will blank out the other important sounds in the environment.

A large room or hall can give opportunities for freer movement. For children with visual impairments it may be necessary to include some landmarks and clues to help with orientation. A careful examination of the room is needed to make sure that all obstacles have been removed. Sometimes, because of the familiarity of a room, an obvious obstacle can be missed. The floor should be slip-proof and, for children with visual impairments, glare-free. Children who do not see well or at all will need to examine the room. This will involve walking them all round the room, examining the walls, learning the position of the doors. This will be followed by accompanying the child across the space, which can be a frightening experience for a child (for example, the sound of the space is different in the middle of a large room from the outside) and developing a feel of the size of the space. The children may find it difficult to assess the actual size of the room and may need a good deal of time to familiarize themselves with the space before they are ready to move independently. At first they may be reluctant to leave the security of the walls and sensitive encouragement may be needed to get them to do so. It may be helpful to identify the different corners of the room with brightly coloured objects. These should also have different sounds and textures to help the child who does not see at all. If the space is a large one, 'markers' can also be placed halfway along the longest walls. Young children are unlikely to be alone in such a space, but it can increase their feeling of security and independence to be able to tell for themselves exactly where they are, without having to rely on other children or adults.

The outside environment

Children should be introduced to the outside environment as early as possible in their lives. It is such an exciting place to be. There are hundreds of new sights, sounds, feels and smells to experience. The weather itself produces a range of new situations; the sight and feel of the sun, wind, rain and snow. It can, however, be very frightening. This different feel to the outside, which may seem very strange after the confines of the house, can lead, initially, to a feeling of insecurity. The sounds of traffic, aeroplanes and so on may startle young children. If the family is fortunate enough to have a garden, the children can learn to explore it as soon as they are able to crawl. This will familiarize them with the experience of the outside environment. Even when they are still in their prams and pushchairs, the children can be shown so much about the outside environment through a short walk along the road. Once the children are walking, a 20-yard walk can become a great learning experience. The children can experience the different sensations of walking on paving stones, on asphalt and on grass. They can feel hedges, walls, railings and fences. Children with visual impairments need to feel these things to understand them. Some children with physical disabilities who travel in wheelchairs may not have had the opportunity to experience the environment first-hand. The experience of feeling them will add much to their understanding and the same is true of children with learning disabilities. You cannot assume these children are absorbing the information and extra time spent in examining the environment will add to their understanding.

The pavement itself is full of exciting objects, such as trees, lamp posts, pelican road crossings, telephone and letter boxes. There are the kerb and the drain holes to examine. Children with visual impairments can be encouraged to develop their listening skills. 'Is that a car coming, or a lorry? Is it coming nearer or going further away?' The different experience of walking under a bridge can be felt and heard. The children can be shown how to use echoes. The sounds that are all around reflect echoes from objects in the environment. Children who have severe visual impairments can start by clapping their hands, stamping their feet or clicking their fingers as they walk through a tunnel or under a bridge. They will begin to appreciate the echo. Gradually their use of this skill will develop. Mobility specialists at a school for visually impaired children devised this game to refine this skill yet further.

> Tell the child that you have a magic switch which can electrify a wall. Ask the child to walk up to the wall and stop as near to it without touching it. Then the child can say the password, the electricity is turned off and the child can touch it. If the wall is touched by mistake, a noise can be made to indicate an electric shock. To begin with let the child have a protective arm out in front. Later this will not be necessary. Any other idea can be used instead of the 'electric shock' if this is not appropriate for a particular child.
>
> All of these experiences and new concepts will be important for the children's mobility and orientation later on and such activities will also provide opportunities for the children to improve and refine the use of their other senses.   (Linden Lodge School)

Creative parents and teachers will think of many other ideas.

EARLY SKILLS FOR CHILDREN WITH VISUAL IMPAIRMENTS

There are some specific skills which can usefully be taught early to children with visual impairments. If the body protection technique can be incorporated into the children's repertoire of movement skills, it will enable the children to guard against the worst of the 'bumps and bruises' mentioned earlier. The second group of skills described below will provide the children with the basics for negotiating the environment.

Body protection

Children with visual impairments will naturally hold their hands in front of them as a means of protecting their bodies. This is not the most efficient way of protection as little of the body is actually being protected. In addition, the children do not appear in control when walking this way. There are two recognized ways of protecting the body.

Upper body protection.   Raise the arm level with the shoulder, the forearm across the body so that the fingertips reach a point just outside the opposite shoulder. The palm of the hand faces the front and the forearm is angled slightly forward to lessen the shock of impact (Figure 2.1).

Figure 2.1

Lower body protection. The hand is held in the centre of the body, the fingertips pointing downwards, and the back of the hand leading.

These techniques may be used together, if required.

Young children with visual impairments should also be taught to be careful in other situations. For example, they may try to stand up when they are under a table. They can be taught to reach up with their hands to see if there is anything in the way of their heads before they stand up. Skills such as this will make the children feel more in control of themselves and the environment.

Negotiating the environment

The following skills will enable the children to begin to make sense of the space around them.

Trailing

When walking alongside a wall, have the back of the hand in contact with the wall, the fingers lightly curved to avoid jamming them in openings, and the arm reaching forward so that the hand is ahead of the body. Walk fairly close to the wall.

Direction-taking

In order to navigate within the environment, it is necessary to be able to ensure that the correct direction is being taken. One way to do this is to locate the direction through reference to a fixed point or to sounds.

Lining up   To line-up with an object place at least one part of the body, such as the shoulder, arm or leg (for a wall), or the side of the foot (for a grass or paving line), against a fixed object. The traveller can then start walking in the desired direction, even when losing contact with the object.

Squaring off   To move at right angles to a sound or an object the traveller must be square to it. To square-off to an object, both shoulders (for a wall), or both toes or heels (for a kerb or grass line) are placed against an object. Alternatively, the traveller's back can be placed against a door, table or similar object. The line of travel can then be determined.

Room familiarization

Exploration of a strange room must start from a fixed reference point, such as the door. Trail round each of the four walls in turn. Locate and identify all objects around the walls. Then explore the space between, starting from the door and moving to the opposite wall. After each crossing of the room is completed, move a couple of paces to the side before starting the next run, until the whole of the floor area is covered. The position of the fixed reference point should be kept in mind. Children can be asked to point to it as they move around the room. Locate and identify all objects within the room and their relationship to each other and to the reference point. Employ any protective measures that may be necessary.

It may be appropriate to use models to explain to children the position of various objects in the room. More information about this is given in the chapter on orientation.

Early route learning

Earlier in this chapter, the excitement of the outside world for the young child was described. It was suggested how much could be learnt through a short walk with the child. Once the child is confident in moving in the outside environment, they can begin to take responsibility for the route taking. Obviously, at such a young age, this will never be done unaccompanied. This section describes a more formal walk on which the children are introduced to the skills of route making. Young children are capable of doing this. The writer recalls asking one 4-year-old blind boy to show her his very large garden. He said 'You pretend you are blind and I'll take you round', which he did, describing the features of the garden and explaining how he knew where he was.

While an adult is holding the child's hand, it is clearly difficult for the child to feel any real responsibility for their own movement. They may enjoy the environment and demonstrate some knowledge about it. However, it is not until they are walking by themselves that they really understand the importance of listening carefully, of identifying and understanding the landmarks. Once they have experienced this feeling of responsibility, they will be far more ready to absorb the information given to them and regard it as important, rather than simply as an interesting and enjoyable adjunct to a walk. On the other hand, children must always be safe and feel secure. They will meet challenges and learn to overcome them, but this must always be based within this feeling of security. Moving around should always be enjoyable and fun, and the carer and teacher must be creative in making it so.

The principles of teaching a route indoors or outside are the same. Examine the route carefully first. Avoid routes that have any dangers and particular difficulties. These can be introduced gradually later, once the children have developed some confidence in moving around. Then examine the route for useful landmarks and any clues (see Chapter 5). Taking the child by the hand, walk him or her along the route, pointing out landmarks, noting any changes in texture underfoot and slopes up or down. Do this several times. When you feel that the child is beginning to recognize the route, walk backwards in front of the child, encouraging them towards you, reminding them of landmarks to watch out for. Be careful to avoid too much of a memory load for the child. As the child develops in confidence, you can walk behind the child, leaving the child to spot and talk about the landmarks. The support given is then gradually reduced as you increase the distance between you and the child. This is a difficult stage for the child as she or he begins to take more and more self-responsibility. You need a very sensitive awareness to be able to judge the right time to do this. If it is done too soon, before the child is ready, it may frighten the child or evoke a sense of failure. If it is left too late, the child may never make the important transition. You remain a longer distance away from the child, speak less and give less feed-back. The child should never be allowed to fail. In any case, disorientated wandering is not helpful, but the opportunity to practise recovery skills and to problem-solve must be included.

An aspect which needs to be remembered is that children with visual impairments may not understand the connection between routes. At the nursery school they may have learnt the route from the classroom to the toilet and from the classroom to the hall, but they may not understand the relationship of the toilet to the hall (Figure 2.2).

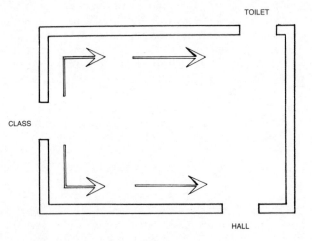

Figure 2.2

Similarly, when trailing a large room such as a hall, they may not appreciate the quickest way back to the door (Figure 2.3).

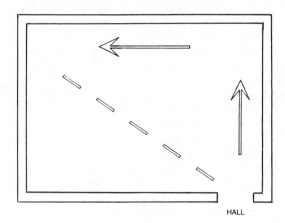

Figure 2.3

Children who are given these route-making experiences have a real basis for future mobility training. Not only will they have developed confidence in navigation, but they will also have learnt some problem-solving skills. When the child is older, the time will come when she or he either asks to, or can be persuaded to walk a route unaccompanied. This is a great day for the child and a major stepping stone to real independence.

When to introduce the cane

There are differing points of view among mobility specialists as to when the long cane should be introduced. Some specialists feel that it should be introduced when the child is very young, while others prefer to leave introducing it until children are 11 or 12 years old. There are good reasons for both points of view. Against introducing it early is that if the children develop bad habits when using the cane it will be difficult to eradicate them later. Another reason given is that learning to use the cane will interfere with the children's use of the other senses. A third reason is that children may regard the cane as a toy and not take the use of it seriously enough. There is validity in all these arguments. However, the writer agrees with Willoughby (1979), who argues strongly for the early introduction of the cane. The reasons for this point of view can be summarized as follows:

1 All life skills are more easily learnt if they are begun early in childhood. Two-year-olds who start exploring with a cane will quickly make it an extension of their bodies. It will also become a natural part of life.
2 If the introduction of the cane is left until later, it may be associated with the traumatic realization of being blind. Furthermore, the cane will be an add-on to the skills they have already developed rather than being an integral part of them.
3 Mobility is very limited without a protective device and can become very boring.
4 Obstacles are easily detected without bruises.
5 Steps are easily detected.
6 Unnatural groping and shuffling are avoided.
7 Normal speed is possible and expected. Walking in a straight line is easier with a quicker speed and there is less possibility of veering.
8 Fear is minimized using a cane.
9 The cane can be taught as a game and fun.
10 Lessons can always be challenging.

11 Taking problem-solving strategies is easier, because there is a longer stopping distance.
12 Using a cane does not rule out direct touching and feeling. Indeed the cane is likely to find interesting objects that the child can stop and explore as it is much more efficient than the hands for investigating the space in front.

Skellenger and Hill (1991) conducted a survey of 37 orientation and mobility specialists who worked with pre-school children. The results showed that 81 per cent of the specialists had given instruction in the long cane or other cane devices to 220 pre-school children. Half of the children had begun using a cane before they were 4 years old and the other half were between 4 and 5 years old. However, nearly 80 per cent of the children had used the cane only under instruction, though some of the specialists had recommended that the children use the cane with the support of another adult. All the mobility specialists reported that the children had increased in the confidence they showed in the mobility and orientation programmes.

Pre-cane devices

A recent development for pre-school children is the pre-cane device. This came initially from the USA with some work by Dr Everett Hill at Vanderbilt University. It has been used by several mobility teachers in America and also by teachers of pre-school children in Sweden.

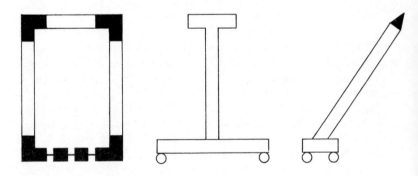

Figure 2.4 *Three types of pre-cane device*

As can be seen from Figure 2.4 these 'canes' can be of various shapes. They are made either from heavy wall schedule 40 PVC pipe or the thin wall variety. The former should be used if durability is the main consideration. However, the device will be heavier and less flexible than if made from the thin wall PVC. Either types of piping can be bought from the local builders' merchants. For all the shapes of devices shown in the diagram, ten feet of piping will be sufficient. As well as the piping, it will be necessary to buy solvent cleaner, some PVC cement and the necessary joints and couplings. The PVC can be cut using any fine-tooth saw such as a hacksaw or even a power jig saw with a fine-tooth blade. The rough plastic edges left from the saw cut can be smoothed off with a knife or a file. It will be necessary to assemble the devices on a flat surface to ensure alignment of the parts. Once the shape of the device has been decided, cut the pipe to the plan, apply the PVC cement liberally and insert the pipe into the joint with a slight twist, holding in place for 15 to 20 seconds.

The easy construction makes it possible to design a form of device that is suitable for each individual child and of course, as the child grows, the device can be exchanged for a longer one. These 'canes' are suitable for the children to use as soon as they can walk confidently. They can start with a device which rolls along the floor on the piping base. As they gain in confidence and control of their device, wheels can be added, either at a central point or on a bar at the bottom of the cane. They are light for the little ones to manoeuvre and the shapes can be easier to hold with two hands. This encourages the children to keep their hands at the midline position, ready for the long cane technique later. Using foam or soft cloths fastened to the handle can encourage correct hand placement, which will nearly approximate with the hand position used with the long cane.

The Hoople

This is a device recently devised by mobility specialists at the Royal National College, Hereford. It began as an aid to students from abroad, where there is a rough terrain which is unsuitable for using the cane. Gibbs (1994) used it with children of 6 and 7 years of age. Her work suggests that younger children might also find it useful. The Hoople is very much like a hoop with one side which can be 'squeezed in' to make a handle; the shape is very much like a large tennis racket with a wide handle. It can easily be made from tubular plastic adapted from the type of hoop used in physical education activities. The hoop protects the width of the body and is then held close to the centre of the body at waist height. On smooth surfaces, the Hoople can be slid along the ground and on rough surfaces a bouncing action is used. Although the information received through the Hoople is not as detailed as that from other pre-cane devices, it is certainly a viable alternative. Gibbs felt that in the play area of her school, which was a large grassed area, the Hoople would be helpful. She found that, after a short programme of teaching with two children, their confidence in independent travel markedly increased.

How to introduce the cane

If the children have been used to pushing a cart around the home, the introduction of the cane will be relatively straightforward. They need to be told that the cane is something special that will help them move around to find things. It must be introduced as a fun activity. Introduce the cane to the child as a giant finger or, depending on the current fashion at the time, it can also be introduced as part of a television, comic or film character, which can almost guarantee acceptance. At the beginning, the children hold the cane in front of them and slide it along the floor. When they come into contact with something, this can be examined and delight expressed at the 'clever magic finger'. The children can tap on different surfaces, walls, metal radiators, doors, listening to the different sounds and can practise finding different floor textures, for example the mat near the front door. They can listen to the different sounds that the cane makes when it is being tapped in an enclosed space and when it is being tapped in a large space, such as a hall.

The teaching of the long cane should always be just part of an individual lesson or part of the week's programme of lessons. While the children are concentrating on managing the cane and making sense of the information that they are getting from it, remember not to overload them by asking them to orientate themselves in space or to process information that is coming to them through their other senses. At the beginning of the programme, the cane can be held with both hands if the children feel more comfortable. This is also a helpful way of encouraging the children to hold the cane centrally, rather than out to one side or the other. When the children have the dexterity and hand control to manoeuvre the cane in a relaxed way, then the swing can be introduced. The children can be shown how to slide the cane from side to side. This must be done, in the initial stages, on a smooth floor surface. The cane needs to be kept in touch with the floor surface. A rough texture makes this almost impossible to manage, without a great deal of experience. Gradually the children will begin to integrate the use of their cane with the information through the other senses. Learning to control the cane takes concentration and lessons should be very short in duration and preferably followed with some free movement for relaxation and to develop and extend the movement skills.

What about the children who have some useful residual vision? Should they be taught and encouraged to use any of the cane devices? A careful assessment through observation should supply the answer. What is the children's posture and walking gait like? Do they watch their feet, or the walking surface much of the time? How confidently and quickly do they walk? Can they detect stairs and kerbs? Can they avoid obstacles in their path? As they grow older they may find a symbol cane sufficient, but there is no reason why they should not use a cane if they enjoy doing so. They will discard it later if it is not needed.

Parents and the cane programme

Parents should be involved with all the stages of the mobility programme and this includes the use of the cane. Their attitude to the child using the cane will be very important and the following suggestions are made to parents.

1 Ask to be involved with any mobility training that is being carried out. Learn the basic technique with your child and expect to be involved with the lessons.
2 Do not worry about the attitude of the general public. They will be very impressed with your child's use of the cane and you will become increasingly proud of his or her achievements.
3 Do some training of your family and friends.
4 Do make it part of your child's life. Going out? Take the cane in the same way as you would take the child's glasses or gloves. Of course, the day the child first has the cane, don't expect them to use it all the time. Nevertheless, it should quickly be built into the day's routine. At the beginning use the cane a little every day, and do not expect, at first, the precise technique described in Chapter 4.
5 Do not anticipate for your child what the cane will be telling them. For example you do not need to, nor should you, tell them that there is a lamp post coming up. This is what the cane is for. They will come to rely on you and what you are telling them, rather than what their cane is telling them. Of course, if your child has not learnt to detect stairs, it will be necessary to warn him or her, but more important, perhaps, is to learn the safety positions for the adult involved in mobility training and put these into operation.

6 Help your child to learn to use the cane with consideration for others. This includes swinging it (though students of mine were found using canes as fencing foils), using the pop-up procedure, and stowing it away in buses and so on.
7 Do use sighted guides sparingly. It is slower to do this than to let your child walk independently, but your child's progress will repay all the time spent doing so. Keep in mind the ultimate aim and draw up some more reserves of patience.

The first few years of the lives of children with special needs are so important. Much of what they achieve depends on this early period. Although this remark, made by an orientation and mobility specialist, refers to a child with a visual impairment, it could equally apply to all children with special needs:

> I would like to turn the time clock back many years and begin to teach the young blind child things he should have learned when he was 2, 3, and 4 years old.   (Webster, 1977)

Mobility and orientation in the school years

Once children enter school, there is a whole new world to explore and to understand. There are also many new skills to learn. Up to this stage, children will have been learning about their environment in an informal way. The school years will be the time when, for most children, the formal education in mobility skills and orientation to the environment begins. To the young entrant, the school building will be a very large and confusing place. This is true for all children and more so for children with disabilities. There will need to be an initial orientation to the school and a gradual learning of all the school buildings and surroundings. Input from a mobility specialist will be of great assistance in teaching special skills. A whole-school policy to ensure the children have opportunities to practise and use their skills will be needed. With appropriate programmes, it is probable that by the time the young people leave school, many of them will have achieved independent travel.

The school environment

As has been noted in an earlier chapter, an appropriate environment is a crucial factor in enabling the children to move independently. Providing this requires the commitment of administrators, governors, headteachers and school staff to the principle of the importance of encouraging pupils' independent travel. The competing interests for finances in schools may make this commitment difficult, but it is helpful to understand, first, that improving the environment for children with special needs will improve it for all the children and all those who work within the school, and secondly, there are many ways to make the environment more accessible which have no financial implications. For example, most schools have a rule that everyone will walk on one side of the corridors, the left or right. If this rule is strictly adhered to, children who have a difficulty in moving, for whatever reason, will have the security of knowing that their line of travel will be easier than if they are having to make their way against pupils coming in the other direction.

Discussions among the school staff and attention to the environment can often provide similar solutions.

A whole-school policy

It is important to realize that mobility and orientation education in school is not only the responsibility of the mobility specialist. In this crucial area of children's development and learning, everyone must be involved. Mobility is not just a matter of specialist training that takes place in a one-to-one session on perhaps two mornings a week. All staff must encourage it and support the training. This includes the headteacher, teaching and non-teaching staff, and must also include everyone who has dealings with the child, such as the people involved in the provision of transport, meals and so on.

First, the children's mobility must be developed and used throughout the week. The mobility lessons or physiotherapy sessions will be used for teaching new skills and new routes. A certain amount of practice of these will obviously be included during the lessons. However, the main practice takes place during the rest of the week as the children go about their day-to-day routines. Swallow and Huebner (1987) suggest that the sequence of learning in independence skills follows three steps: learning a specific skill; the incorporation of the skill into the daily routine; and the application of the skill as needed. The application of the skill and the incorporation of it into the daily routine are the responsibility of the school. The physiotherapist may have introduced a new way of moving for the child with a physical disability. The mobility specialist may have taught the child the route from the classroom to the dining room. However, incorporating this into the daily routine and encouraging the child to use the route when appropriate must be encouraged and developed by the school staff.

A whole-school policy for mobility skills will also ensure that the children are guided in the correct operation of the techniques learnt. For example, if members of the school staff are aware of the right way to hold and use a long cane, they can remind the children if they either forget what the technique is or do not remember to use it. A simple comment, quietly spoken, such as 'Duncan, you're swinging the cane too far to the left', can be very helpful. If Duncan is severely visually impaired, he may not realize that he is not handling the cane correctly. If Jeannie is looking confused at a corridor intersection, a comment such as 'Jeannie, can you remember what you have to think about to find Mrs Fould's classroom?' will prompt the child with learning difficulties. Such reminders will support the work of the mobility specialists, and will prevent the children from becoming habituated in unhelpful techniques or movements. As a result, the new skills will become automatic more quickly. This type of help requires more than an understanding of the principles underlying mobility education. There has to be real collaboration between the teachers of mobility and the rest of the staff. The mobility specialists must be prepared to share their expertise and the staff must be prepared to listen. The mobility programme needs a regular review and update, so that all are aware of what stage the child has reached.

A third major reason for the whole-school policy is that children can sometimes play one member of staff off against another. If the children do not want to use their mobility skills they may try to persuade members of staff or other pupils that they are unable to do certain tasks. The writer well remembers a member of staff in a school where a blind girl, Lucy, was placed. Lucy's mobility skills were developing well, and she was well able to get herself around the school and playground independently. However, she was not very keen on doing so. It was noticed that each morning when Lucy arrived at school, the staff member carefully lifted her out of the taxi and carried her into the building. Lucy loved this and the member of staff was fully persuaded that Lucy could not get into school by herself. It was unfortunate that the staff member paid more attention to what Lucy said than to the mobility specialist.

Preparations before arrival at school

Preparations will be needed before the children arrive at their first school and again when they transfer from one school to another. A critical preparation will be that of training for staff. In a special school for visually impaired pupils, where the majority of staff will be qualified to teach these children, there will be an understanding of and a commitment to the principles of mobility education. In addition, there is likely to be a mobility specialist at the school on a regular basis. Special schools for children with physical disabilities or with learning difficulties will ensure that the staff are shown how to lift and move these children appropriately. Unfortunately, as has been suggested, there is little general awareness in mainstream schools of programmes to develop these skills. Furthermore, in these schools there may be no one who is there all the time or who visits regularly who has the expertise in these helping strategies. Part of the in-service training that the staff receive in order to help them with all the areas of the curriculum should include some input on mobility and orientation. The elements that should be included in this training are discussed more fully later in this chapter.

Preparations for children with visual impairments should include arrangements for them to visit the school campus before the official starting date and to have some orientation training. These visits will provide opportunities for the children to start learning some specific routes, for example, how to get from the classroom to the gymnasium or from the cloakroom to the science block. Some pupils will need several visits to the school. Arranging these visits will require the co-operation of the school and the parents.

A further preparation which should be made before children with special needs arrive at the school will be making any modifications to the environment that are required.

Attitudes of staff

One of the most important factors in developing mobility and orientation skills in children during their school years will be the attitude of the school staff. A theoretical whole-school policy is only the first step. To be of real benefit the policy needs to be put into practice. It is to be hoped that all the staff will be convinced of the importance of this area of the special curriculum. One example of an unhelpful attitude has been described earlier. An example of a positive attitude would be the understanding by staff of pupils who are late for lessons, because they have been travelling across the campus independently. Moving around a mainstream campus, particularly a large complex one, will take longer for pupils who are physically disabled or visually impaired than for their peers without disabilities. Annoying as it is for teachers to have the start of their lessons interrupted by late arrivals, this understanding is important. There will also need to be arrangements made for the timing of actual mobility lessons and again understanding will be needed by class and subject teachers. There is, increasingly in schools, extreme pressure on the timetable. The demands of the National Curriculum and all it involves mean there is little space in the curriculum for pupils with special needs, such as for training in the use of residual vision, or independence skills. Staff may be very reluctant to allow these pupils to miss lessons in specific subjects, especially if they appreciate the amount of time that is needed for these pupils to access the main curriculum, but time must be made for mobility lessons. Within the primary school timetable, this is probably relatively easy to arrange, but it may be more difficult in the secondary schools. In addition, there is often a tendency to suggest that mobility and orientation lessons for children with visual impairments should take place in physical education or art lesson times. This may also be true of children with other special needs. The rationale for using these subject lesson times is frequently that the pupils are unable to take a full part in these areas of the curriculum. However, these subjects are very important for all pupils and should not be missed, certainly not on a regular basis. There may be an argument for the occasional physical education period to be used for mobility, for example when the rest of the class is doing formal ball games such as football, but for pupils with special needs these physical activities are as important if not more so, than for the other members of the class. The aesthetic and creative aspects of art, drama and other similar subjects have their importance for pupils with special needs. As so much of the school lives of pupils with special needs demands extra effort and concentration, these areas are needed to provide a holistic balance for them.

A suggestion that is often made is that mobility lessons should take place during lunch times. This is not really satisfactory. The pupils will already have been working as hard as if not harder than their peers in the morning lessons. They need time to relax, not being made to work in mobility lessons. In addition, the break times are an important time for developing social relationships and this opportunity should not be taken away from pupils with special needs. The staff, together with the mobility teacher, must decide on the best possible timetable arrangements for mobility lessons, so that the pupils do not miss the same curriculum lesson nor are denied times of relaxation.

The attitude of teachers to mobility lessons is also critical. One member of staff was heard to say 'Oh, you're off out again, are you? Enjoy yourself!' and another, a teacher of mathematics, was heard to comment 'You're back. Come on, buck up, there's a lot of work to finish.' This particular comment was made as the writer returned with a young man who had just spent 40 minutes learning to negotiate a busy road crossing. Both of us had been working hard and felt more like having a sit-down and a cup of coffee than settling down to some mathematics. One-to-one mobility lessons are a concentrated period of time. The work is mentally demanding and physically tiring, and the pupil needs to have a few minutes to draw breath rather than return to immediate pressure. The time allotted to mobility lessons is often so short that the mobility teacher is unable to allow a few minutes' relaxation before the pupil returns to the classroom. The understanding of teachers can make an important difference.

In-service training

The staff of a school have a right to some in-service training before they are asked to work with a pupil with special needs. It is clear that teachers in mainstream schools, who will have had little or no experience with pupils who have physical disabilities or who are visually impaired, have a particular need for such training. This can possibly be provided by physiotherapists, by the local education service for visually impaired people, or by staff from a special school which is meeting the needs of the particular pupils with special needs. This training should include information on mobility and orientation skills. It is most likely that some of the training sessions will include experiential work, such as using wheelchairs or participating in activities under blindfold and simulating spectacles. It should never be suggested that such activities will give the users the actual experience of being disabled, as simulations can never convey the whole implications of a physical disability or a specific eye defect. However, using them for specific tasks does give some idea of the particular difficulties of an activity for someone who does have a disability and of the effort and concentration needed to complete a task, and also the need for appropriate helping strategies, allowing users to begin to devise some specific ways of overcoming the difficulties. In terms of mobility and orientation, having the experience of being under a blindfold or simulating spectacles and being guided by someone who is not efficient, careful or confident can be invaluable. The fear of moving without vision is quickly understood, as is the importance of efficient guiding. The experience can also demonstrate the amount of concentration required and the resulting tension and fatigue that is felt by many travellers who are visually impaired. Hopefully, the training session will include the basic principles of guiding, and instruction will also be given on the techniques which were described in Chapter 1. As has already been noted, there are many people besides teaching staff who will be involved with the pupils. All of these people should also be included in any in-service training sessions.

Preparation for school trips

One aspect of the whole-school policy will be the preparations and the arrangements which are made for school trips. There are various types of these, such as visits to museums, field trips for geography and school leisure outings. Whether these be for pupils with special needs from special or mainstream schools, the mobility aspects of the visit must be considered. The following questions can be a guide:

- Are there any access problems with the visit?
- Are there any particularly difficult parts of the trip for the pupil's mobility? For example, a visit to a castle may require a climb up a steep grassy bank. Castles also have steep staircases and slippery paths in the dungeons. All these are great fun and the children

should have the opportunity to visit such places, but some pupils may require assistance for parts of the visit.

- Will the pupils need their own individual adult helper? This isn't automatically necessary, and will depend on the age, ability, disability and mobility skills of the pupil with special needs and the peer support that is available. However, if an individual helper is not going to be present, close attention must be paid to the various activities of the day in case help will be needed in any specific situations.
- Would it help if the pupils were introduced to the layout of the area to be visited prior to the trip?
- Should a tactile or large print map be prepared? This will depend on the individual pupil and may or may not be helpful.
- When going out on visits with pupils with special needs, it is sensible to warn the 'hosts' beforehand. They are usually very willing to 'bend the rules' a little for pupils with special needs; the writer well remembers the ecstatic expression on the face of a blind 5-year-old who was specially allowed to hold a falcon on his wrist. Even where physical access causes problems, the staff will often help to overcome these.

Escort duty

The lack of movement opportunities for many children with special needs may also be exacerbated by the fact that those in residential schools do not have to walk to school and those attending day schools are mainly transported by taxis. This restricts not only the development of their physical skills, especially stamina, it also restricts their day-to-day experience of the environment.

A new and exciting development in the teaching of mobility and orientation skills to pupils with visual impairments has been the arrangements that some schools are making for bringing the children in to school. Instead of the children being brought in by taxi, they have their own individual escorts who come to the house each morning and take them to school. The children and escorts use the most appropriate routes, travelling on buses and trains where necessary.

This enables the children to become accustomed to the route in a very natural way. When the children's mobility and orientation skills are at the required standard for travelling the route independently, they are taught it by the mobility teacher. Many pupils travel to school independently as a result. Of course, this programme of 'escort duty' is only possible where the pupils live either near the school or near to a bus route. But this successful programme demonstrates the initiatives that can be taken through the development of a whole-school policy. Such a programme could well be extended to pupils with learning difficulties.

The role of the class and subject teacher

The teachers who are involved with the pupil, either as class or as subject teachers, have a critical role to play in the development of mobility and orientation skills.

They are involved with the pupil on a daily basis and have the opportunity to observe their mobility and orientation skills in practise. The teachers can assess how independent the pupils are, how far they rely on their peers, and whether they have an adventurous or nervous personality. All this information is vital to the mobility teacher, who may only see the pupil once or twice a week, or even less regularly. Once the mobility specialist has initiated the individual programme and has started teaching the pupil some specific skills or routes, the class and subject teachers are the people who will be able to comment on how far a technique has been acquired and how far it is being used in the day-to-day situation. A teacher of young children described the following incident: a 4-year-old blind child was asked to go to the first school, as opposed to the nursery unit, to ask for some flour for the baking session. This was the first time the child had travelled this route alone. Previously he had always had an adult with him. A message had already gone to the first school, via the internal phone, so he was expected. He arrived safely, gave the message, but took longer to make the return journey than was expected. When he eventually returned he was grinning from ear to ear with his success. The reason for the delayed return was that on the return journey he had been unable to open one of the doors so had returned to ask one of the first school staff for help. As the teacher said, this was real problem-solving and both she and the boy eagerly awaited the arrival of the mobility specialist the next day to impart the news.

A teacher of pupils with physical disabilities felt that to develop the young people's responsibility for themselves and their sense of adventure and exploration were the most important means he had to develop the independence of his secondary-aged pupils.

These two examples demonstrate very different attitudes from that of the teacher who said 'As long as the children know how to get from the door to their desk, that's all that's necessary'. This shows a lack of understanding of the needs of the pupils, particularly those with visual impairments, with whom he dealt. When, as sighted people, we walk into a strange room, we can quickly orientate ourselves through vision. We see, at a glance, the shape and size of the room, what sort of furniture there is, how it is arranged and where other people are sitting. This helps us feel comfortable in our surroundings. All pupils with visual impairments should be taught room familiarization techniques and given the opportunity to use these in every room that they use. Children in wheelchairs can be shown the easiest way to negotiate a classroom.

As far as possible, all pupils should be given responsibility for looking after their own books, materials and equipment. This is as true for pupils with special needs as for other pupils. However, this will depend on the accessibility of cupboards and so on, as well as the physical capabilities of the individual pupil. In addition, unless they are shown where cupboards and other storage spaces are, pupils with visual impairments will not be able to take this responsibility. They will then be dependent on the teachers or their peers and may resist taking responsibility in the future.

The class and subject teachers also have an important role in developing positive attitudes in the other pupils. A balance must be found between encouraging them to be kind and helpful and allowing them to do everything for the pupil with special needs. One teacher was required to deal very firmly with a class of young children who fought for the right to hold the hand of a child with learning difficulties. He was not allowed to move a step by himself without another child grabbing his hand. The teacher was anxious not to destroy the attitude behind the action, but to moderate the behaviour. The personality of the child or young person will determine to a very large extent how supportive the peer group will be. Some children and young people naturally attract the support of their peers, while others seem to deter help. Teachers can mediate between the children and young people with special needs and their peers, fostering interdependent relationships.

Cross-curricular issues

The teaching and encouragement of mobility and orientation skills, and particularly of the concepts involved in this area, are the responsibility of all the class and subject teachers who are involved with the child. Many of the opportunities for developing the concepts occur naturally within the daily routine and within subject teaching. It may be necessary to highlight these for the pupils with special needs who may not appreciate the relationship between what they are doing in, for example, mathematics, and what they do in mobility lessons. In addition, many of these pupils will find it difficult to generalize from many of the concepts they learn. For this to be done successfully, the subject teachers need to have a thorough knowledge of the concepts involved in mobility and orientation and, more particularly, a knowledge of which stage the children have reached in their programme of mobility. A summary of some of the ways that different subjects can be used to increase the pupil's concept understanding is given below. This is not an exhaustive list by any means. Teachers, together with the mobility specialist, will be able to provide a comprehensive list for their own subject area.

Movement, physical education, dance

There are marvellous opportunities for developing both mobility and orientation aspects of independent travel in these curriculum areas. Lowenfeld (1971) suggests that the education of movement improves and feeds into children's ability to learn academic subjects. This is true for all children, especially those with visual impairments. Walker (1992) states that 'visually impaired children need to experience physical and outdoor activities as much, if not more than sighted children'. Tooze (1981) is also clear that the physical education curriculum is an important part of mobility education.

Unfortunately, children with special needs are too often left out of the areas of physical activity and are frequently expected to use the time for catching up on other work. This must not happen. Mobility education is a strenuous activity and the children need to be fit to take the fullest advantage of it. In addition, physical activities develop the body awareness needed to follow the instructions given in route taking, and they need to have good posture to be able to walk in a straight line without veering. All the lessons involved with movement will help develop these skills. For young children there is the chance to develop the gross motor skills: running, hopping, jumping, skipping and learning how to negotiate the simpler pieces of equipment. Young pupils should be encouraged to swing on ropes, walk along forms and bars and use trampolines. All of these will enable the children to gain an understanding of how their bodies can move and to increase their control over their movements. One of the factors in walking that children with visual impairments find difficult is the transference of weight and balance from one foot to the other. The varied activities which movement lessons involve will help to develop this in an informal and enjoyable manner. The other normal activities of a movement lesson for young children will also be appropriate. These include curling up small and stretching, walking on tiptoe or very slowly, stretching the foot, feeling each part touching the floor. Tooze (1981) also encouraged her pupils to jump off forms or boxes, pointing out that jumping into space was a skill that would be required when the children alighted from trains or buses.

As the children progress through school, the physical education curriculum changes to include more sophisticated skills, such as ball games and the use of more complex equipment. Participation in the formal sports such as football, netball and so on may be difficult to provide for pupils with special needs. The majority of them will never be able to compete on equal terms with their peers. However, gymnastics, athletics and swimming should pose few problems which cannot be overcome. The writer recalls a young woman with a severe visual impairment who represented her school in the county's gymnastics competition and came second.

Dance is a marvellous activity for children with visual impairments and the best form of this is patterned or sequenced dancing such as country dancing. The repetitive movements and the boundaries that such dancing provides are very helpful. In addition, the partner and group aspect of the activity gives the children with special needs a real opportunity to work with other children.

Physical education within school should be only part of the programme. Children with special needs should be encouraged to take part in physical activities out of school, and opportunities made available to do so. There is no limit to what it is possible for these youngsters to do. Walker (1992) in her book describes young people who are visually impaired taking part in a wide variety of activities such as orienteering, horse riding, mountaineering, canoeing, skiing and caving; this list can be extended to just about anything. Walker's book is a useful basis for teachers of physical education and those involved in leisure activities who are working with pupils who are visually impaired.

Teachers of physical education who are working with pupils with special needs can get advice on how to help these pupils from their local educational advisory services, and advice from therapists will also be needed. A useful booklet *Games for All of Us* is available from the Royal National Institute for the Blind.

Drama

The skills used in mobility and orientation can be developed in the curriculum area of drama. The more informal lessons develop the body image and self-concept of children and give the opportunity to use their bodies in a fluid and controlled manner. Both in individual, paired and group activities, children and young people can learn to express themselves through their body language. This is often particularly difficult for pupils with visual impairments. They do not see other people's gestures and movements and their lack of vision hinders their free movement. In the controlled environment of the drama lesson, children and young people can enjoy expressing themselves. Role-play sessions in drama give all pupils, both with and without special needs, the opportunity to practise situations that form part of the interactions between both groups in general society. When travelling independently in their locality, young people with disabilities find themselves in a variety of interactions with the general public. There will be times when they need to ask for help, for example while shopping or on public transport, when they need help in finding specific bus stops. There will also be times when the young people need to refuse offers of help, for example when the offers are inappropriate or when they feel that help is not needed. It is likely to be during adolescence that pupils meet the general public in situations which they have to manage themselves. It is also at this stage of their lives that many adolescents find communication skills difficult. Role play can give them the opportunity to practise these skills. It also gives the fully sighted pupils the opportunity to 'try out' the situations experienced by their peers with special needs.

In the more formal presentations of drama, pupils with special needs can contribute on an equal footing with their sighted peers. The stages for the production of plays are small and the pupils can learn stage directions (incidentally, this skill can feed into specific orientation lessons) and take a full and enjoyable part in drama productions.

Mathematics

Initially, there may seem little connection between learning to travel within the environment and the subject of mathematics. However, many of the concepts learnt in mathematics have direct relevance to the mobility and orientation aspects of independent travel. The environment is based on a series of shapes and patterns. An understanding of shapes, such as circles, squares, triangles and so on, can help children understand how buildings are constructed. These concepts of shape can also be used to explain road layouts, town and village plans and shopping centres. For example an introduction to a new building is far more easily explained with a description such as 'This building is rectangular with a square on one side'. Angles are also important and can be a method for explaining changes in direction. Once the children understand geometrical concepts, instructions such as 'Make a turn to 45 degrees' can give very precise information.

There are many other concepts in mathematics which also feed into the children's understanding of the environment. Travelling in the environment involves the concept of distance, discussed in Chapter 5. For pupils with visual impairments understanding distance includes understanding measurement and speed. These pupils' concept of distance is understood through the amount of time it takes to reach a destination. Their knowledge of a measurement such as 100 metres will be based initially on the fact that this takes a long time to walk. The work in mathematics will give them a more objective idea of 100 metres. The mobility teacher can then use measurement terms in teaching routes. Comparison of different measurements will help children when they begin to build up their own routes and when they use maps and map scales.

Science

The National Curriculum documents for science in the early stages state that 'pupils should be introduced to ideas about how to keep healthy through exercise, personal hygiene, rest and personal safety'. This sets the mobility and orientation curriculum right within the science curriculum. The children's concept learning in science will be necessary for their understanding of their work in mobility, and vice versa. Experimentation and problem-solving will develop the children's mental skills which they will need for successful independent travel. The study of human biology will increase their understanding of their bodies and how they work and the higher levels of chemistry and physics will add to the young people's total understanding of the world around them.

Geography and environmental studies

Geography and environmental studies are clearly areas in which orientation is developed. In their mobility lessons, the children will have been learning about their immediate environment and how to negotiate it.

They will have been using and making maps for themselves. Without this practical experience it may be difficult for them to understand the larger area, or the maps of unfamiliar locations. Geography will give them the opportunity to study the wider locality and extend their knowledge to other countries. It will also increase their knowledge of specific concepts which are needed for mobility. Work on the compass and compass points will be an invaluable aid to both the pupils and those working with them on orientation. The field trips which form an important part of the geography curriculum will give them the opportunity to extend their use of their practical mobility skills.

Craft and design technology

A teacher of this subject expressed his commitment to mobility in this way. He identified the skills needed for the visually impaired child to operate successfully in his department:

- moving safely in a particular environment;
- being independent in that environment;
- able to find and return equipment;
- able to move equipment.

This teacher then discussed the ways in which he tried to develop these skills within his classroom.

1 Children with a visual impairment are shown how to get to seats around the main working table and are warned of the dangers within the immediate vicinity.
2 The children are given the opportunity to make an organized search of the room, starting with the perimeter of the room. This demands organized language from the teacher and a considerable effort of memory from the children.
3 Using the particular subject of craft and design, the children build a model of the room, using Lego bricks. This is an activity followed by all the children.
4 Even when children seem comfortable in the room and all this input has taken place, it is always necessary to watch for the pupil who is temporarily lost and to call out some appropriate instruction so they can re-orientate themselves.
5 The teacher then assesses the children by asking them to go to certain parts of the room (for a reason, of course).

The teacher points out that the encouragement of independence in finding tools and materials is probably the biggest time saver.

The above examples are just a few ways in which the concepts needed in mobility and orientation can and should be developed by class and subject teachers. It is not a comprehensive list. Once the awareness of the teachers has been raised, any and every subject will provide opportunities for both concept development and for practising mobility skills.

The mobility specialist

The attitude of the school staff to the area of mobility and orientation can be shown by the attitude they take to the mobility teacher. In special schools the mobility teacher will almost certainly be a full-time member of staff and have the full support of all colleagues. In mainstream schools, however, the mobility specialist will almost certainly be coming into the school on a sessional basis, once or twice a week. It is difficult in this situation, unless real efforts are made by the school staff, for the specialist to feel a real part of the life of the school. The role of the mobility specialist may not be understood by the staff in the school, and there may not be time for discussion to take place between the specialist and the other staff. This can make the mobility specialist feel very isolated and under-valued. Mobility is a fascinating area to teach, with so many aspects involved in it, but lessons do require a considerable amount of patience on the teacher's part and it is often very much a waiting game. The teacher must hide any feelings of frustration at the time it takes a child to move even a little way, and must accept feeling tired while she or he has to stand and wait while the child makes an examination of a doorway. With older pupils who are working out-side, the weather plays its part. Being enthusiastic about walking along a long street in the pouring rain may be difficult, particularly as the walking pace is likely to be slow! A high level of concentra-tion is needed by the adult in watching for the safety aspects, carry-ing out continual observation and assessment and entering into the learning experiences of the child. Some teachers, who are unaware of what is involved in teaching mobility and orientation, have com-mented that the role is a 'soft option'. It isn't!

Working with parents

Communication with parents is one area of school life which all schools should and do take seriously. It is worth noting here that the whole-school policy for mobility and orientation should be part of the ethos of the school which is communicated to parents. This demonstrates the commitment of the school to this area of the spe-cial curriculum which will encourage the parents to take it seriously and will be supportive to the pupil and the mobility specialist. If there is a waiting area in the school for parents and other visitors, this can be used to display leaflets on mobility. Leaflets can be obtained from the Royal National Institute for the Blind and include *How to Guide a Person with a Visual Impairment*, which gives useful information for the general public on helping people with visual impairments.

It will probably be the mobility specialist who will give the par-ents detailed information on their child's mobility programme. Indeed one of the roles of the mobility specialist is to work closely with the parents.

However, if all staff know of the programme they can give infor-mation to the parents, should the mobility specialist not be available, and of course many children with visual impairments still do not have access to a mobility specialist, in which case the school will be responsible for discussing this area with the parents.

Assessment

There are several ways in which the children can be assessed for their levels of achievement in mobility and orientation. These assessment methods can be either formal or informal. The formal assessment procedures for children with visual impairments would include the use of tests and checklists, some of which have been tried out with a large number of these children over many years. An example of these is the Cratty and Sams Body Image Test (1968), which is reproduced in Appendix 1. It is not only useful for children with visual impairments, but also gives those working with children with learning or physical difficulties a very good idea of the children's understanding of body concepts. Equally, there are several tests devised for use with children with learning difficulties, which would prove of value to mobility specialists. Other assessment checklists are those which have been devised by mobility specialists themselves (see appendices). These can be very useful in that they can help teachers structure their observation of the child. A disadvantage of these is that the mobility specialist has probably devised the checklist around his or her own situation. This will mean that the checklist will include routes which are location specific; these will need adapting to the individual situation. Other checklists are so general in nature that they give little more than a list of aspects for assessment. Examples of these are also included in the appendices. Most mobility specialists use a combination of checklists and a route assessment list which is specific to their own school situation, which they have devised. It is useful for the mobility specialist to have access to a number of these different procedures which they can then adapt for their own use. The main form of assessment will be that of observation and this will take place both during the lesson and outside it.

The ability to make close and careful observation is the hallmark of a good mobility specialist and there will be very few moments during a mobility lesson when the pupils are not being observed. The information gained through this observation will tell the specialist whether a new skill has really been acquired or whether concentrating on a new skill, perhaps that of using hearing more effectively, has led to a lowering of the standard of another skill, such as the use of the cane. Observation will show the specialist what clues the pupils are using. Are they tending to use the information they receive through the tactile sense more than using the sounds around them? It is helpful if the specialist observes the children both when the latter are aware of it and when they are not. For most of the time during the lesson, the specialist will be observing as a natural part of their role and the children will probably be unaware of it. However, it can give additional information if the children are sometimes told that they are being observed. The comment 'I'm going to watch you very carefully today. I shall be looking at your posture while you are walking' can often bring an immediate improvement in the way the children hold themselves and the way they walk. The results may surprise the teacher. One young man whose posture the writer criticized during a mobility lesson said 'I didn't think it mattered. I didn't think you were looking!' This spontaneous comment led to a long discussion about looking, seeing, presentation skills, the need to have good posture for one's health, and so on. It also showed the importance of really listening to the pupils' own comments. The one-to-one relationship during mobility lessons allows the opportunity for such issues to arise and to be discussed. Any assessment procedure must also take into account what the pupils say themselves. They need to have the chance to discuss their views of their strengths and difficulties, which in reality may differ from the view of the teacher. The pupils must be given the opportunity to discuss their progress, to plan the next stage of the programme and to share their feelings about the whole subject of independent travel.

Although the mobility specialists will be observing and assessing the pupils all the way through lessons, there need to be regular occasions when information from parents and the rest of the staff can be incorporated. The assessment needs to be continual and multi-disciplinary. It will include all aspects of mobility, from the use of pre-cane skills to the negotiation of road crossings, from the younger children finding their way to the front door, to the young people crossing the city centre.

The mobility lesson

The mobility lesson will have several aspects to it and some of these, such as preventing fear and problem-solving, have already been discussed in an earlier chapter. There are other important principles that may appear to be fairly obvious but which are so important that they need to be made clear.

Motivation

The need for giving children reasons to move is crucial. The mobility teacher must put great emphasis, when planning the lesson, on the motivational factors for each individual pupil, and as far as possible these must be incorporated within the lesson. Although practice of the sub-skills involved in independent travel will be needed, this can still include some reason that the child understands. The lesson can be a treasure hunt, the mobility teacher having hidden some 'treasure' beforehand. The booklet *Mobility Ideas* (RNIB) includes many useful suggestions.

All lessons should be enjoyable and fun. Mobility training is very hard work, requiring a great deal of concentration on behalf of the child and the adult. Children must enjoy doing mobility, otherwise it will be impossible to keep them motivated to move and their ability to concentrate and to learn will suffer. The one-to-one aspect of mobility training may be difficult for both adult and child and demands high levels of concentration from both. As a change from individual lessons, it can be helpful to consider activities that can be done by more than one child. An example of this would be the examination of a new area, listening to traffic noise, or visiting the shops. The safety aspects must always be kept in mind and some activities will only be possible while working with only one child.

The developmental age of the pupil

The lesson must fit the developmental level of the child or young person. There are no set ages when one skill or another must be accomplished and all children will have their own starting and finishing point for a programme. The development of skills will probably follow the same progression, but not necessarily so. Some children, because of their difficulties, will find the mobility side of this education easy, while others will not. Some children will find understanding space easy, others will not. In addition, within each of these areas, children will differ as to their understanding of the different topics. There will be pupils whose listening skills are well developed and who perhaps have always taken an interest in sound. These children will enjoy lessons on traffic flows and identifying different vehicles. Other pupils with poor listening skills or who are afraid of traffic will find this part of the programme very difficult. However, the adults' in-depth knowledge of the children will provide the mobility specialist with a basis for intervention, and careful observation of the children during mobility activities will enable the mobility specialist to compile an individual profile.

Length and timing of the lesson

The length of a lesson and the timing of different activities within it are also clearly important. For a 5-year-old, ten minutes is usually long enough for one activity and there needs to be variety within the lesson which should probably not exceed 20–30 minutes. For pupils who may be older, stronger and used to the hard work of mobility lessons, a longer period of time may be possible. Indeed it may be necessary. As the routes, particularly the external ones, become longer, the time taken to execute them will of course be longer. In addition, visits to areas in the locality such as the local shopping centre will involve travelling time.

Ensuring success

An important principle for mobility lessons will be to ensure that the pupil meets with success at some point during the lesson. Each route of travel and each lesson is planned for success to prepare the learner for the next route of travel. Self-confidence is slowly developed in the visually impaired traveller as they overcome the restrictions of their environment by this sequential lesson planning. The traveller is never asked to attempt a skill that is beyond their present level of ability, but the lesson should also include some problem-solving situations and some challenges which need to be overcome. The teacher will be able to judge how much of this to include in any one lesson.

Progress will not be constant

It is important to remember that, as with any aspect of the pupil's learning and development, progress will not be uniform. It is often a case of two steps forward and one back (rather an apt phrase for mobility!). Individual lessons will be affected by the pupil's feelings on that particular day, their degree of tiredness, the time of day or minor illnesses such as the onset of a cold; all these will affect the level of motivation, powers of concentration and so on. The mobility session may follow a spelling or mathematics test, and to expect full concentration on the mobility may be asking the impossible. In addition, the level of performance itself will vary during the lesson. It is probable that at the beginning of the lesson, the pupil's movement will be fluent and the use of the long cane, if included, will be good. As the lesson progresses, and the child gets tired and is asked to concentrate on the orientation aspects or the use of the other senses, the cane technique will falter. Similarly, when the cane technique is the focus of the lesson, the pupil is unlikely to make the most efficient use of the other senses and may not be able to concentrate on exactly where he or she is. Judgement must be used to decide which is the main objective at any point during the lesson. However, it has to be said that some children may try and find a way of getting out of the hard work of a mobility lesson. A 9-year-old convinced many of the staff in his school that his understanding of space was very poor, until one day when he heard his mother was in school. He very quickly found his way to the headteacher's office. Genuine fear must always be taken into account, of course, and this is another case where in-depth knowledge of the child is vital.

Constituents of a lesson

Planning an individual lesson should be made with the above principles in mind and should also include as many of the following aspects as possible: assessment, concept development, the use of language and terminology, the use of the other senses, mobility skills, orientation, free movement, and problem-solving. It is probably not possible to include each one in every lesson, but every aspect should receive attention over the space of a few lessons.

CONCLUSION

For most children with special needs the major part of their mobility and orientation education will take place during their school years.

—4—
Mobility skills

INTRODUCTION

Much of this chapter is concerned with the mobility skills which children and young people with visual impairments need in order to travel independently and much of it may not be applicable to children with other special needs. Some of the basic skills were described in Chapter 2, in the discussion of the young child, as it is to be hoped that the first skills are taught when the children are young. However, each child needs to be assessed for his or her level of skill and a programme implemented accordingly. If the basic skills have not been learnt, the teaching programme should obviously start with these. It may be that some of the more advanced skills, such as the long cane, have also been introduced to the children. This will probably have been on an informal basis. However, there comes a time when these techniques need to be refined.

This chapter begins with a consideration of how to develop an effective use of the other senses for the child with visual impairments and then goes on to describe the specific techniques which will be used by these pupils to travel safely in the environment.

USE OF THE OTHER SENSES

Hearing

One of the myths that the general public often has about blind children is that their sense of hearing is more advanced than that of sighted children. This is not so, as hearing tests of both groups confirm, and in many cases children with severe visual impairments use their hearing less effectively than their sighted peers. This is because the visual feedback that sighted children receive increases their understanding of what they hear. However, children with visual impairments can be taught to use their hearing more effectively and this is particularly important for their independent travel skills. Some blind children use their hearing to a very sophisticated level and are able to detect lamp-posts that they pass on the street. The reason they can do this is because they know what to listen for. They detect the change in pitch of the sound waves bouncing off the wall as they walk down a corridor. When they pass an open door, there is no surface nearby for the sound waves to bounce back from. Although the change in sound is a very subtle one, some children are able to detect it. The same thing occurs when the children walk towards a wall. As they get closer, the sound changes and helps them sense it. This skill isn't hard to learn, but to be really proficient at it requires a lot of practice. Some children with little or no sight do it automatically. If this is so, it is helpful to point out to them what they are doing, which will then refine the skill even further.

There are two experiments you can try which will demonstrate this skill. Find the smallest room in your house. Close the door – and your eyes – and either speak or clap your hands. Remember what the sound of that room is like. Now go to the largest room in the house and stand in the middle and make the same sound. The difference is very noticeable. If you could go into a gymnasium and stand in the middle, you would hear a very open sound. The sound there would have a long distance to go to bounce off the walls and return to your ears.

The second experiment involves sound shadows. We all know how a shadow is created by the sun; if we stand with our backs to the sun, we see the shadow in front of us as our bodies block the sun's rays. The same phenomenon occurs with sounds. Turn on a radio and place it on a table. Walk several paces away from the radio, then turn around and face the radio. Take a piece of cardboard and hold it between you and the radio. You are now standing in a sound shadow. The cardboard blocks the sound waves that are coming from the radio. Any time there is an object between a person and a sound, it creates a noticeable sound shadow. The larger the object, the larger the sound shadow. This is how children with severe visual impairments can learn to tell where bus stops, trees and parked cars are situated and where there are gaps in walls. As well as by sound, the end of a building can be detected by the feel of the air that is encountered at the end of a building line. Again, training in these skills should be started when children are young, and activities for introducing these were described in Chapter 2.

The weather will interfere with the use of children's hearing outside. Strong wind or rain will distort the echoes that are received. Snow has a very deadening effect on environmental sounds and is known as the 'blind man's fog'. Unless this is understood, the children's difficulties will not be understood. As the children develop their listening abilities, they can learn how to interpret the sounds of traffic.

Traffic sounds

Learning how to understand traffic sounds is of extreme importance for the traveller with severe visual impairments. Although there are activities which can be done in the classroom or elsewhere inside to train listening skills, the best classroom for learning about traffic sounds is out on the pavements. The training can be introduced very informally. Take the pupils to a street. Have them listen to a car start and pull away from a kerb. Explain that some cars travel beside them, whereas at a junction, cars will travel from left to right or vice versa. Have them listen to the sound of a car as it stops at a stop sign, as it idles at traffic lights, and so on.

The different aspects of using traffic sounds include:

- locating a main road by the sound of heavy traffic
- identifying the direction of traffic sounds
- judging the distance of the traffic by the sound
- walking along a road using the sound of a stream of cars as a guide, going with the sound and against it
- locating bus shelters by traffic sounds.

Use of residual vision

Corn (1989) highlights the difficulties in orientation and mobility for children with low vision. She identified various differences in the ways that the sighted public interact with low vision individuals as compared with individuals with functional or total loss of sight. These differences include the fact that the needs of people with low vision are often the same as those of blind people but that the needs for the former often go unnoticed. This is true in many aspects of the lives of individuals with low vision. Alternatively, as Corn points out, the needs of blind and low vision individuals may be different but are assumed to be the same. Because they are able to function visually in one situation, for example walking along a pavement, the need for help in crossing the road is not understood. A further point is that some mobility needs of low vision people are unique to the 'experience of having low vision'. For example, the vision of the individual may change from day to day, or hour to hour. The sighted public may find this extremely difficult to understand and may even accuse the low vision individual of faking, or even cheating. Comments such as 'He could see all right this morning, what's different now?' are fairly common. However, individuals with conditions such as diabetic retinopathy do find that their vision does vary.

Many children and young people are helped to use their vision effectively through the provision of a low vision aid. This is an optical device which provides magnification. There is a variety of such devices, but the main one used in mobility and orientation is the telescope aid. A telescope, as most readers will appreciate, gives a very restricted field of vision. The main way in which a telescope will aid a traveller would be as a spotting device (Jose, 1983), which can help the traveller see street names, bus numbers, road signs and so on. The children should be assessed by a low vision specialist who could prescribe the most suitable telescope. However, low vision specialists are not always available and finding the appropriate aid may be a matter of trial and error for the mobility specialist and the pupil. The child will need training in how to hold, focus and use the telescope and this may take time. Jose suggests several activities to develop this skill and points out that to use a telescope efficiently the user needs to use head movements, rather than eye movements. This may take some while to accomplish. It is important to note that the telescope must be used in conjunction with other visual skills. A child will need to know how to locate the street signs or bus numbers before he or she is actually able to use the telescope to read them.

Children with partial sight can be shown how to use their vision in the most constructive way for them as individuals. For example, they may not be able to see far enough to tell where the tills are in a supermarket, nor, if they are in a strange locality, what the particular procedures are for that shop. But they can look out for people with full trolleys and follow them, which will get them to the checkout point. They can then watch the people in front of them to learn where to place their baskets, where to get the carrier bags from, and so on. Many partially sighted children are not attentive observers and often miss the information-giving gestures and movements of others. They can also have explained to them how to structure, cognitively, the environment from certain visual clues. If they do not have sufficient vision to detect steps at ground level, there may be other visual clues which they can see which would also give them a clue that steps are near. Colour, for those children who are able to see it, can help to make sense of the environment. Various shop signs, McDonald's for example, may be seen and other shops could be identified from their relative position to it.

This involves a great deal of structured observation of the children, watching them as they move around. It should also involve the mobility teacher discussing with the children what they see, what this might mean, and creating opportunities to see if they were correct in their assumptions. If the assumptions made by the children are right, this will help them to build a vocabulary of 'visual clues' which they can then use in other, unfamiliar situations. If they are incorrect in the conclusions they reach or are unable to draw any implications from what they saw, this will lead on naturally to a teaching programme. This should enable children with low vision to develop a problem-solving dimension to their work in mobility and orientation, which will be critical as they begin to move through different localities without support from adults.

Time should always be spent within a lesson developing the pleasurable side of using vision. I have always been concerned that children are expected to use their vision for work-focused activities, whether academic or mobility and orientation lessons. This is very natural on the part of teacher, parents and others. However, the best motivation for using vision is the pleasure it gives. If we can manage to give children pleasure and joy from looking, it will encourage them to persevere with the frequently painful, distressing and fatiguing consequences of struggling to use their sight.

The use of the blindfold

You may think that to introduce a blindfold to a young person with low vision would be totally inadvisable. In the majority of cases this is so, but there are isolated instances when its use may be helpful. Some young people have 'night blindness', a rather incorrect term describing the difficulties with seeing in poor light which some eye conditions, such as retinitis pigmentosa, cause. It may be helpful to use the blindfold to demonstrate to the young person that their cane techniques are sufficiently safe to be trusted. There may also be occasions where the young person struggles to make sense of visual images which may be very poor, and this interferes with the information which is being received through the cane, the hearing and so on. Using a blindfold may perhaps alleviate this confusion. I recall a young man for whom this was certainly true. Rashid's posture and normal walking gait were poor. His walking speed was slow and there was no difficulty in identifying him from some distance away simply from his posture and gait. His mobility teacher asked Rashid to show me how he moved when wearing a blindfold. The change was dramatic. Rashid's posture and walking speed improved and it was difficult to identify him from the crowd around him, unless one spotted the cane. Rashid said he felt very confident under a blindfold. However, the implications of this example would need discussion with all concerned, especially the young people themselves, before using a blindfold in similar situations.

The use of the tactile sense

Children and young people with severe visual impairments rely heavily on their tactile sense. In terms of mobility and orientation, they will need to obtain information through their hands and their feet. Teachers and parents are likely to put an emphasis on developing the use of the children's hands. It is recognized how important these will be for understanding the environment and for reading Braille, should this be required. There are many books and leaflets which give suggestions for activities to encourage children to use their hands more effectively. In mobility and orientation, the children will use their hands for exploring the objects around them, the different surfaces they encounter and, later on, for reading tactile maps and diagrams. Perhaps the same emphasis is not put on the development of the tactile abilities of the feet, but being able to discriminate between different walking surfaces, or changes in ground level, and to detect gradients is essential for independent travel. If children are not experienced in using their feet in this way, specific teaching programmes will be needed. This may start with the children using their bare feet in an indoor and safe environment.

The development in the use of the other senses will go alongside the teaching of the more advanced skills used in mobility.

EXTENDED SKILLS

The basic skills of trailing, room familiarization and so on have been described in Chapter 2. This chapter describes the more advanced techniques that will be taught to many of the children and young people. These are skills which, for children with visual impairments, go hand in hand with the work on orientation which will be discussed in Chapter 5. Some children will never achieve all the techniques, but they may be able to achieve individual aspects within them. One student will be at the stage of being led down a quiet hallway learning to understand the information received through the cane. Another will be travelling by bus to the local shopping area, locating the right shop, making a purchase, returning to the bus stop and catching the right bus back to the starting destination. It does not matter which stage the students are at. Every stage of the programme is important for the individual child or young person. Even if they can't achieve each stage independently, they may be able to negotiate parts of the specific skill and this is all part of increasing the knowledge and quality of life of the children and young people.

Teaching the following techniques is usually and preferably undertaken by a mobility specialist. However, if such a professional is not available, the following description of the techniques should enable a teacher to start showing the pupil how to use the cane. Even where there is input from a specialist, it is helpful for teachers and all those working with the child or young person to understand the techniques of mobility. The mobility specialist will not be there all the time. Encouragement, guidance and specific instruction can support the particular stage of the programme, and will also help the pupil's development in the correct techniques and prevent the formation of bad habits.

One essential element of the teacher's role in teaching these skills is to keep the pupil safe. There are prescribed places where the teacher should stand while teaching each technique. Sometimes, the teacher can become so involved in observing the pupil that, perhaps momentarily, the safety aspect is forgotten and the teacher finds him or herself in the wrong location to ensure the safety of the pupil. Every care must be taken to see that this does not occur.

Introduction of the long cane

The use of the cane may well have been introduced to the child at a young age and have already been accepted by him or her as a normal part of the day's routine. If this is so, half the battle is won. However, the child may not be using the cane in the safest and most efficient way and it may be necessary to explain that to make travel really safe, there are some 'grown-up' ways of using the cane, which you feel the child is ready to learn.

If the cane is being introduced for the first time, children may well show resistance to the idea. The idea of the long cane sends very definite messages to a child or young person, the latter particularly. If this situation is not handled very sensitively, the message can be heard as 'You are blind – you must identify yourself by carrying this cane. You cannot move around without using one.' These thoughts may have been in the back of the young person's mind for some time and the suggestion of the cane may well bring all the fears out into the open. Alternatively, the young person may not have ever considered the possibility of being regarded as blind and may find the suggestion shocking and traumatic.

Before any suggestion of using a cane is made, the feelings and expectations of the child or young person need to be explored. There also needs to be consultation with the parents and other teachers. It may be that at the same time as the introduction of the cane is being considered, other teachers are also considering the possibility of introducing Braille, which is likely to be another emotive suggestion as far as the young person is concerned. Specific counselling may be necessary if the young person is to be helped appropriately.

A full assessment is essential before the introduction of the long cane. This assessment will include a consideration of the child's motor, concept and language development. The child's previous experience and current level of motivation will also need to be taken into account. The proposed programme can then be adapted to take account of these, with particular attention being given to the areas where the child has difficulty. If the assessment is to be comprehensive, parents and staff in the school or college must all be consulted.

You need to know that the child understands your instructions; the language you use will have to vary with the age and ability of the pupil. Calling the cane a 'giant's finger' may be appropriate for a 6-year-old, but not for a 14-year-old. Children display different strengths and acquire skills at different rates. A 5-year-old may take several months to achieve an approximation of the cane technique, whereas an older child may grasp it quite quickly (even though continued practice would still be necessary). Some children will grasp the mobility skills side of independent travel quickly; others will find understanding the environment easier than the negotiation of the cane.

Figure 4.1

The cane's main use is a buffer to protect against collision. It may be used also as a probe, to check the area in front, and to identify obstacles (Figure 4.1). If the cane is not held correctly, full protection will not be afforded. Although the aim is for a relaxed and easy posture, holding the cane at first will feel uncomfortable and cause tension. At this stage, it is easy to slip into a lazy technique which does not prevent bumping into objects and prevents the detection of changes in ground texture and, more critically, where there are changes in ground level.

Figure 4.2

Teaching

Stand behind the child, clasp the fingers over the cane and place the child's arm into the central position (Figure 4.2). Explain to the child what you are doing. Walk a few steps with the child as you help him or her to hold the cane high and centrally. The child can try a few steps alone, just pushing the cane in front. Confidence will soon come and then finding obstacles can be introduced as a game. The pupil is told that there will be obstacles and that the cane will detect them. As soon as the cane detects an obstacle the child is to 'freeze'. The object can then be examined. A similar procedure can be followed for changes in ground surface, such as mats in front of external doors (these are important as orientation clues).

The next stage in the mastery of the cane is detecting drops in the walking surface and the position of the teacher while this is being learnt is crucial. The teacher must stand in front of the pupil one or two stairs down, in case the pupil fails to stop or happens to trip.

When children can detect obstacles and drops, they can be shown how to slide the cane from side to side in a small arc. One way of demonstrating the feel of the correct technique is to move the child through an exaggerated wrong action as a contrast. Once the child is walking confidently with the cane, unexpected obstacles can be placed in the child's path. When this is first introduced, the child would be allowed to examine the obstacle with the cane and/or the

Figure 4.3

hands, but the pupil should gradually be encouraged to detect the obstacle, work a way around it and carry on. In the environment there are going to be countless obstacles, and if examining every one becomes a habit, progress along a route is going to be slow indeed. When the child is walking with the cane, the adult must take care to walk in a place where safety can be ensured. This may be in front of the child, in which case the adult will need to walk backwards, or it may be possible to walk behind the child. Both positions will also be helpful in monitoring the child's gait and posture.

Possible difficulties and teaching strategies

The child may experience some difficulties in the use of the cane. Some of the common ones are described below, with suggestions for teaching strategies which may be helpful.

1 *The pupil's posture and walking gait are poor.* When pupils are first learning to walk with the cane, the posture and gait often deteriorate, or it may be that the pupils have never developed a good walking posture. There is a need for lots of free movement in secure surroundings. It may help, too, if the adult walks with the pupil, with the latter holding on with their free arm. This may give the pupil just the extra bit of confidence needed to walk more freely. The use of the child or young person's imagination can be an invaluable aid. Suggestions can be made as to who the child

could walk like, and these suggestions will of course depend on the age and interest of the pupil. One young woman of 15 changed her walking posture dramatically when I asked her to walk like 'Lady Di', imagining that she was wearing a gorgeous dress. We were also able to use this to improve her posture when walking down the stairs. She said she was imagining that she was in a palace walking down a huge staircase with everyone waiting for her.

2 *When looking for something on the right side (assuming the cane is in the right hand), the child extends the entire arm out to the right*, thus covering a large amount of floor space, with the danger of interfering with the travel of other people. One school of thought advises the use of a short cane in this situation. However, this tends to make the stiff extended arm a part of the reach, which is not advisable. Instead, insist that the child keeps the forearm against their waist, centring the hand and using only hand and wrist movements to direct the cane. Then the arm cannot be flailed out to the side. Tell the child 'If you need to reach farther than your cane can reach, then turn and move in that direction. People expect you to move forward, not sideways.'

3 *The pupil insists on holding the free arm out in front* as if to feel with it, particularly when obstacles are detected. This can be prevented by asking the pupil to use both hands on the cane for a little while, which will prove to them that the cane can be trusted to detect obstacles in front of it.

4 *The pupil continues to resist the cane.* The importance of sensitivity to the feelings of the child, the young person and the family has already been stressed. Additional strategies for the young child might include giving the cane a name, and, for the older pupil, stressing how good they look using it and rewards for having the cane with them. One strategy that might be appropriate would be to involve the pupil with a friend who is an efficient cane user and ask the latter to demonstrate how helpful the use of the cane can be.

5 *The pupil does not understand instructions.* As with many other areas of education, terminology has crept into mobility and orientation. Jargon must be kept to the minimum and the emphasis must be on practical demonstration and the child learning by doing. Any terminology that is used may need translating for children, particularly younger ones. It should also be introduced gradually.

If the children are introduced to the terms 'inner and outer shoreline', they will understand any mobility teacher who uses these phrases. However, confusion may be caused by teachers using different words to describe the environment. A simple example of this was where a child was asked to 'walk until your cane finds the asphalt' by one teacher and 'walk until your cane finds the Tarmac' by another.

One important word to use carefully is the word 'right'. This is often used to mean 'correct', 'ready?' or 'do you understand?'. As can be easily seen, this can cause great confusion when the words and concepts 'left' and 'right' are being used and in situations where the teacher is giving the child directions.

Diagonal technique

The diagonal technique means the cane is held in the usual grip, but the arm is extended straight ahead and the hand turned, so that the tip of the cane extends outward and downwards, resting on the floor and just outside the opposite foot. The crook of the cane turns outwards and protects the knuckles of the cane hand.

In most programmes of training in the use of the cane, the first technique that is usually taught is the diagonal technique. This is used when moving in a familiar indoor environment. This may be appropriate for the adult who has become visually impaired.

For children and young people, there may be good reasons for not teaching this technique early. Children who have used the long cane from a very early age or who have used pre-canes (see Chapter 2) may find learning to hold the cane in the diagonal technique feels awkward and uncomfortable. Other children or young people, who have never held a cane before, have probably been negotiating the indoor environment at school or at home very well without any sort of aid. Indeed, many children know their surroundings so well that they are able to race around without any difficulty. I had the experience of reprimanding a blind boy for running in school, needing to remind him to consider the needs of other not so confident pupils, and of course the staff. This particular pupil, and there are many others, would find it frustrating and pointless to learn a technique to be used in a situation in which they already feel confident and comfortable. It may be sensible to go straight to the touch technique, which is generally used outside, and teach the diagonal technique at a later stage. In this way the lessons have an immediate purpose, and later the young people will realize the advantage of the diagonal technique. So, although the various published mobility programmes suggest more or less the same order of skill teaching, this order must always take into account the needs, strengths, previous experience and motivation of the individual. Clearly, there is some hierarchy of skills, but there are many adaptations to programmes which can be made without affecting this.

As with the use of the long cane, this method does not protect the entire body from all obstacles, but it protects most of it from the most unpleasant ones. It is used to protect the user from the unexpected – furniture temporarily sited in corridors, and so on.

Walking in a straight line

If early intervention programmes have been in place, most children and young people with visual impairments will have no problems with maintaining a straight line while they are walking. The children will have enjoyed plenty of free movement, walking, running and so on. They will also have been shown how to stand with the body held in alignment and they will have experienced how this feels. Children who have not had this demonstrated to them may not be able to stand with all their body held correctly. For example, their feet may be facing slightly to the left while their shoulders and head are facing slightly to the right. This will make it very difficult for them to set off in a straight line. These pupils need to get accustomed to the feel of standing straight which can then be extended to walking while maintaining the correct posture. Some pupils will always veer to one side or the other and in this case they need to be reminded to make a conscious effort to correct for this. In addition, any route devised for them will include clues which will tell them when they have done so. For example, if they continually run into the grass on their right, then they should keep a bit more to the left.

Some mobility teachers suggest that children should be encouraged to keep in contact with a wall or fence (sometimes called 'shorelining'), as the means for walking in a straight line. However, this is not necessarily a reliable method for maintaining a straight path. The wall may curve and the pavement may widen or disappear. It is preferable, instead, to teach them to move ahead and simply notice whenever an edge or barrier is encountered. The competent traveller recognizes that following an edge is only one possible means for maintaining a straight path, and mainly relies on walking speedily and consistently while keeping oriented to the environment.

Another question arises in crossing an open area such as a playground. The children should not expect, or be expected, to walk 'straight as an arrow' towards a precise point (for example from the school door to the gate at the other side of the playground). Some correction will almost certainly be needed. In this case, if the child reaches the school and does not immediately find the door, the wall should be followed for a few feet to the left or right, and then the opposite direction tried if necessary. It is reasonable to expect the children to learn to walk in a fairly straight line so that the correction is relatively minor. Walking quickly and confidently is important; the slow and hesitant traveller wobbles and has no clear direction.

Meeting other pedestrians

Once the use of the cane has been mastered in a quiet outdoor environment, the pupil will need to learn to respect the needs of other users of the pavement. When meeting other pedestrians, the pupil should be able to locate them through the sound of their footsteps or their voices and keep to the inner shoreline. If it seems likely that a collision may occur, then it is sensible to stop, draw the cane into the upright position close to the body, until the other people have passed. In addition, if the pupil feels that the other pedestrians are wanting to overtake, it is only courteous to stand aside and let them pass. It might be asked why there should be any chance of a collision when the other person is sighted, but members of the general public are sometimes surprised to see a cane user. There is a tendency for the sighted person to be slightly nonplussed and not quite sure what to do. This is especially true with children, particularly younger ones, who often fall silent in admiration. Speaking to them can often clarify their location. In addition to children, there may be prams, pushchairs, bicycles and toys around. It is safest to proceed cautiously and it is preferable if the pupil can take control of the situation themselves.

Figure 4.4

Accepting and refusing assistance

The majority of people who offer assistance to a cane user will grasp their arm and try to propel the young person in front of them. The young people can develop the art of taking charge of the situation and preventing this. This will be partly through developing good communication skills. But the following strategy can also be adopted. If a member of the public takes the traveller by the arm, the traveller should let the grasped arm go very limp, stand still and gently, but firmly, disengage the hand. If assistance is needed, explain politely why the hand is being disengaged and take the proper hold. Check that the guide understands exactly what help is required. If help is not required, as the grasp is disengaged, thank them and move away.

The cane technique on stairs

Ascending

During instruction in this technique, the adult must take care to remain *behind* and therefore *below* the learner. In this position, should the child stumble, a reassuring arm can be placed on his/her back.

When the tip of the cane locates the first step, the traveller should: Advance until the toes of both feet are touching the step. This ensures that when the first step is taken, the foot will land safely on the stair. Measure the height and width of the step, and the width of the staircase with the cane. Locate the handrail, if any. Position him/herself to one side of the staircase, if appropriate. Make sure the body is square to the first step. Slide the hand down the cane and hold it loosely between the thumb and the first two fingers. With the arm held straight ahead, lift it up so that the tip of the cane is just against the tread of the third step up (Figure 4.4).

As the traveller climbs the stairs, the hand and arm should be kept in the same position so that the cane remains two steps ahead of the feet. This will mean that the cane gives the traveller early information about the top of the staircase. When the tip swings free, there are two more steps to mount. As soon as the tip is free, clear the landing and then resume the normal touch technique after the last step up is taken.

There are a couple of points to be highlighted with the acquisition of this skill.

- Handrails cannot always be relied upon. Many handrails do not extend the full length of the staircase, often stopping short of the level surface at the top and bottom of the stairs. In addition, there

are many flights of stairs where there are no handrails. Travellers should learn to negotiate stairs without the use of rails, if at all possible.
- It is important to square off with the stairs before starting to climb them. Unless the feet are square to the stairs, the traveller may start to ascend at an oblique angle and trouble will ensue very quickly. The best way to avoid this is to place both feet with the toes against the first stair. This also helps to ensure that the whole foot is placed on the stair or step. If the feet are placed away from the stair, there is a danger that the traveller will only put the front of the foot on the stair. The result of this will be that at this or the next step, the traveller will trip up.

Descending

During the instruction of this technique, the adult remains *in front* and therefore *below* the learner. In this way, as when the learner is going up the stairs, the adult can prevent any stumbles or falls. Descending stairs feels more frightening than going up and this fear must be handled sensitively. There is a tendency to go very slowly, which is not helpful. It results in the learner having to balance on one foot, with the danger of over-balancing. If necessary, the learner can come down the stairs one at a time, placing both feet on each stair and pausing before she or he continues.

Figure 4.5

When the drop-off of the first step is located by the cane, the traveller should hold the cane firmly against the riser and advance cautiously to the cane, until the toes just touch the first step. Check the measurements of the stairs, and check that their position is square to the steps. If there is no handrail, drop the free arm close to the side of the body with the cane held loosely in the other hand, the tip just over the edge of the second or third step. If the arm and cane are kept in this position as the descent is made, the tip will touch the ground one, or perhaps two steps ahead (Figure 4.5).

Clear the area in front as soon as contact is made with the ground, and then resume the normal touch technique. When descending, it is helpful if the traveller keeps their weight back a little so that in the event of a stumble he or she sits down safely on the stair. If there are known to be handrails, these can of course be used.

ADVANCED SKILLS

Road crossings

Clearly, crossing the road requires a highly sophisticated level of skill and this depends on the pupils' having achieved the various sub-skills of mobility and orientation which are needed. The input of a mobility specialist will be needed to teach the children and young people these techniques.

There are several ways of crossing roads. The safest one to use is the audible pelican crossing. Unfortunately there are not too many of these around. Zebra crossings can also be negotiated by many children. Road intersections which are governed by traffic lights are more complex. However, these are usually placed at a busy intersection and there will be other people around who can be approached for assistance. Finally there will be many occasions when the traveller needs to cross a road where there is no identified crossing point.

The basic points to remember are as follows:

1 Find the down kerb with the cane.
2 Stand with one foot squared off to the kerb to determine the line of travel, the other placed in a comfortable position a little behind to ensure balance.
3 Hold the cane close in. If held in front, the cane will be in the road and is in danger of being swept away by the traffic!
4 Through listening to the traffic sounds, determine a safe time to cross. Having made the decision and started, carry straight across the road. There may be a temptation to change the mind and dart

back to the safety of the pavement. This should be resisted, however, as it will confuse any drivers who may be approaching. If the traveller's route across the road is made clear, drivers have the opportunity to swerve if necessary.

5 Negotiate the opposite kerb, move away from it and re-take the required direction of travel.

There are three stages in using a pelican or zebra crossing. The crossing must first be located, as it is no use walking along a road hoping to find an audible pelican or zebra crossing. The travellers must know where these are to be found. Secondly, they must also be able to identify the precise spot of the crossing, the particular post with the beacon or box on it. (The writer's own mobility instructor recalls seeing her lovingly stroke several lamp-posts in an attempt to find a pelican crossing which she had temporarily lost.)

After the crossing has been located and identified, it must be negotiated.

Pelican crossing

Stand by the pelican post, facing the traffic. Pelican crossings usually have ramped kerbs, which means that the traveller who is visually impaired cannot determine the line of travel from squaring off on the kerb. The slope to the crossing may give some idea of where to stand, but this will need practice.

Press the button and wait for the 'bleeper' sound.

Cross the road and get to the opposite pavement. The bleeper may stop sounding, but the light continues for several seconds and there is plenty of time to make a crossing.

Zebra crossing

Locate and identify the crossing. Square off to the kerb to determine the line of travel. Decide when traffic is stopped or absent. This requires good listening skills as not only the sound of the nearside traffic needs interpreting, but also the traffic sounds on the opposite side of the road. When the traffic sounds suggest that it is safe to do so, cross. It is also a courtesy for travellers to acknowledge the drivers with a smile or wave.

Indented crossing

Where there is a road intersection, one of two methods can be used. The first is known as an indented crossing (Figure 4.6).

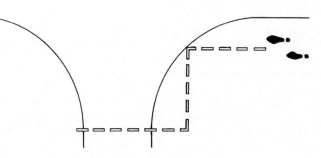

Figure 4.6 *Indented crossing*

The aim of this method is to take the traveller away from the main corner to a position where he or she can square off to the kerb. Taking the line of travel at the corner is likely to take the traveller into the middle of the intersection. Indenting round the corner ensures this doesn't happen. It is only necessary to go a few yards round the corner. At this position, the traveller can be seen by all traffic and there should not be any parked cars in the path of the crossing, which is then negotiated in the manner described above.

As Figure 4.6 shows, this method of crossing consists of a series of turns. In the figure it is shown as a right turn, two left turns and another right turn. It must be remembered that on the return journey, the turns will be reversed, that is, a left turn, two right turns and another left turn. This method of crossing, though a safe one, does rely on the traveller having very good body concepts and also the ability to make accurate right and left turns. Some children and young people will not be able to use this method, simply because of difficulties in this area.

Auditory crossing

The other method of crossing is the auditory crossing. As was stated earlier, it is difficult to line up for a crossing at a road junction as the kerb will be on a curve and no accurate line of travel can be identified. However, people with very good listening skills can line up with the sound of the traffic.

Once the down kerb is detected, pause and listen to the traffic sounds, especially the line of traffic moving on a parallel path (this traffic may obviously be moving in either direction). The sound of the traffic identifies the direction to travel. When the traffic sounds suggest that it is safe to cross, move to and off the kerb and cross.

The use of public transport

The use of public transport can contribute enormously to the independence of any young person with special needs. Indeed, as they reach adulthood, many people who have mobility problems move to a town or a city because of the independence that public transport can give them. Unfortunately, in terms of their general experience and particularly in developing mobility skills, many children and young people undertake most of their transport in cars. Several young people with visual impairments have told me that they have never travelled by bus or train (although some of these had travelled by plane!). There will be young people who will never be able to travel independently by bus or train, but the experience of going on public transport will add enormously to their understanding of the environment and of other people's lives. This programme can be incorporated into the years at school. Even if the pupils only spend one day each half term visiting the town or city centre and using public transport, this can build up into a valuable store of experience.

Bus travel

The skill of being able to use a bus successfully can be divided into the following sub-skills:

1 **Planning the route**, which includes knowing the times, numbers and destinations of buses; knowing the location of the bus stops at either end of the bus journey and being able to negotiate any transfer of buses.
2 **Locating the bus stop**. This will be part of the route-building process. Travellers will clearly need to know where the bus stop is and a landmark should be indicated on the route to help this, using tactile, auditory and visual clues where appropriate.
3 **Locating the entry door to the bus**. Bus drivers do their best, parked cars notwithstanding, to stop the bus with the door close to the bus stop or the entry to the bus shelter. The bustle of passengers alighting, the noise of the doors opening and the change in temperature should also help in locating the door.
4 **Getting on the bus**. The children will probably need a good deal of practice in climbing the steep steps which most buses have. The handrail should be located, as this will help. The general public may well also try to assist by pushing from behind!

5 **Buying a ticket if necessary**. Most children and young people who travel by bus will use a bus pass, but they should be taught how to operate the ticket machine and how to communicate with the bus driver.

6 **Finding a seat**. Many travellers with visual impairments have stories to tell of sitting on another passenger's lap. Coping with embarrassing situations is one important criterion of successful travel. Gently trailing one hand out to the side from the back of one seat to another will usually indicate if a seat is occupied and continued experience of bus travel will develop the skill of being aware of empty seats.

7 **Being able to identify the bus stop required**. Asking the bus driver or other passengers for assistance, 'Please will you tell me when we arrive at the post office?', will normally solve the problem. This request can be forgotten and the children and young people should be shown how to detect progress along the route. This can be done through recognizing particularly busy bus stops, roundabouts, hills and any visual clues, if these are appropriate. It is also important that as part of the training the children examine the bus stops before and after the one required. Then if the children get off at the wrong one they will at least know in which direction they should be walking.

8 **Getting off the bus**. While introducing this to the child, the teacher will stay in front of the child to prevent any falls and will give verbal instructions to guide the child off the bus. Buses do have very steep steps, which can be difficult to negotiate. However, most children prefer to do so themselves, rather than depend on the general public, who may tend to pull them off the bus.

Learning to use a bus can be, as suggested by Tooze (1981), an activity which is done with a group of children. Each of them can be given a different task and responsibility. These different tasks can include: finding out the bus number, asking the driver for tickets, asking the driver to alert the group to the correct bus stop for leaving the bus, following the route the bus takes, and noticing any landmarks. Working as a group in this way can be very motivating and individual children with little or no sight or with learning difficulties can all share in the problem-solving and decision-making.

Train travel

Uslan *et al.* (1990) reported that travellers who were visually impaired listed the following difficulties in travelling by train: entering the station; finding the ticket office and locating the end of any queue; negotiating the money; finding the ticket barrier; making the way to the correct platform; coping with crowds, many of whom are rushing in the opposite direction; getting on the train; exiting on arrival at destination platform, especially deciding on which side of the train the platform is. One traveller added 'And try getting a guide dog through one of those ticket barriers'.

However, many young people do learn to overcome these difficulties and, with a great deal of courage, make regular journeys by train. Using trains will include several of the sub-skills already described under bus travel. Orientation to the railway station will be needed, and moving from the entry point to the ticket barrier and on to the platform will use the basic principles of route making.

Town travel

Once the various skills of using the cane have been mastered, children and young people will enjoy their trips to and through town centres. More of these are becoming pedestrianized, which makes travel safer, though not necessarily easier as there will be no particular line of travel and people may be moving in many different directions. Children and young people who use their residual vision for mobility and orientation may find this confusing. They will need strategies to cope with this more complex situation. If there are a lot of people about, the traveller should keep the cane further in to the body and keep the arc of the swing small. This prevents any possibility of danger to other pedestrians.

If children and young people have any residual vision, they should be shown how to make use of shop signs, hoarding boards and so on to keep themselves orientated.

Additional travel skills

The following descriptions of techniques used in negotiating escalators, lifts and revolving doors should enable parents and teachers to support the learning of the young people.

Escalators

The approach to an escalator should be noted on the route or map which the young person is using, although footsteps or the rumble of the mechanism will often give the clue to its whereabouts. On encountering the metal grid at the entry point, the side of the escalator should be located with the cane; the traveller then reaches with the hand and gently contacts the moving handrail, letting it slide by underneath the hand. The direction of the moving handrail should be checked (is it moving away and not closer?). This ensures that the person does not try to go up a 'down' escalator or vice versa.

Moving onto the metal grid, the arm is extended so that the cane detects the moving step ahead. (An 'up' escalator gives a short, chopped motion to the tip, a 'down' one gives a longer, wavy motion (St Vincent's School).) The cane is held gently against the grid, keeping the tip away from the sides of the step. The click will be heard and felt as each stair join passes under the tip. When going up the escalator, it may be more comfortable to place one foot on the step above, as this feels more balanced. When the steps start to flatten out, be ready to exit. Step forward and clear the stairway.

Lifts

When the lift stops and the doors open, ask if it is going up or down. Enter the lift carefully with the cane in the diagonal, the tip resting on the floor. In most lifts, one enters and leaves by the same door. Care should be taken when leaving, as there may be people immediately outside the door. Use the diagonal technique, sliding the tip along the floor.

Using the lift controls and checking if the floor is the correct one are difficult if the lift is unfamiliar and if there is no one around to assist. Trial and error will be required.

Revolving doors

The characteristic sound of the doors revolving will indicate their location. Moving to the right of the door, the side wall is contacted, and the cane is brought well in against the body. Using the upper hand and forearm technique, contact the edge of the moving doors with the hand.

The thick rubber flaps on the door prevent any danger of trapping the fingers. Locate the edge of the door frame, then stand slightly to the left of it so that the shoulder clears the frame. Maintain contact with the revolving door edge so that the rhythm becomes familiar. When ready, step forward as soon as a door has passed. Follow the door, keeping the forearm in contact with it. Ensure that the cane is close to the body and not liable to foul the doors. The opening on the other side can be detected by sound, temperature changes or air currents. Take a couple of steps away from the opening to give room to anyone behind, then check the path in front before moving off.

The techniques described in this chapter have been included not necessarily as teaching instructions, but so that the principles for each skill can be understood by all those working with and supporting children and young people. Many of the skills would need to be broken down into a series of sub-skills for individual pupils. However, an increase in everyone's understanding can only improve the experience of the children and young people travelling independently.

—5—
Orientation

WHAT IS IT?

As has already been explained, there are two aspects to travelling within and through the environment: mobility – being able to move safely, avoiding drops and obstacles; and orientation – the understanding of space and how one relates to it. It is this latter aspect that is the most difficult, particularly for the child and young person who is congenitally visually impaired or who has severe learning difficulties. Successful orientation depends on spatial knowledge. Spencer *et al.* (1977) emphasize this and write: 'spatial knowledge is, above all, knowledge which facilitates mobility: knowing the location of resources, of places of safety, security and viability; knowing the routes for efficient travel and when necessary for escape.' They further point out that the lack of vision 'throws the individual back onto a much more laborious way of learning about space and integrating this information'.

Orientation is usually no problem to the youngster of average ability who is born with sight. Orientation ability develops so naturally that educators of sighted children scarcely give it a second's thought. It is assumed that when sighted children grow up, they will have learned how to move freely within their homes, neighbourhoods, schools and towns, knowing where they are and how to reach their destination. This assumption is mostly correct. Maintaining orientation is little problem for these sighted children. Even before they begin to crawl and walk, they have already begun to learn about space and to develop their spatial knowledge. Once they are moving, they confirm their knowledge through their explorations. They need no specific intervention to teach them about spatial concepts. However, children with little or no vision or with learning difficulties will need a structured programme of direct teaching if the concepts involved in orientation are to be established.

DIFFICULTIES EXPERIENCED BY CHILDREN WITH SPECIAL NEEDS

Children with a learning difficulty

Children with learning difficulties may well have problems understanding their environment. Many of these children focus on a small area around themselves and their primary care-givers and pay little attention to the areas further away from them. This may restrict their knowledge of the environment. These children may also have difficulties understanding their body concepts and terms such as left and right. The result is that some routes may not be comprehensible to them. They will be able to see landmarks, but may not know what to do with this information. For example, when walking a route, the children may be able to travel to a letter box, but may not understand what to do next, whether to turn left or right. In addition, the memory load of remembering a route may be too great and they may need to have other supporting strategies. These children may well need to follow a structured programme in orientation.

The writer was involved in running workshops for teachers of young people of school-leaving age who had learning difficulties. The teachers had felt that there was something they could do to improve their pupils' travel skills, and they were hoping to teach the young people the routes from school to the nearby adult opportunity centre. The workshops demonstrated that many of the aspects of the programme for young people with visual impairments are applicable to pupils with learning difficulties. The young people needed to learn to identify landmarks, recognize clues, understand traffic flows, negotiate road crossings, make decisions, solve problems and be ready for the unexpected. The result of the workshops was to establish a programme of mobility and orientation for the school leavers. Although some of the programme had been a natural part of the rest of the curriculum, the teachers felt the input had not been sufficient. There needed to be a more identified focus on orientation, which began with the very young children and their body concepts and their free movement. It was felt that this should progress to route planning and execution. The programme should also include the use of their other senses. Many of the children, although they could hear, were not identifying and interpreting these sounds. For safety reasons it was important that they did this. As for many children and young people with visual impairments, totally independent travel may not be a realistic aim for all pupils with severe learning difficulties. However, after the programme had been implemented for the school leavers, several of them made remarkable progress and were able to travel independently in the outside environment. The teachers also noticed that the other pupils had increased their understanding of orientation and that the programme had assisted in giving them some control over their environment.

Children with a physical disability

It is obvious that the mobility aspect of independent travel will be affected for children with physical disabilities. It should also be realized, however, that these children may have a restricted understanding of their environment. This is further discussed in Chapter 6. Teachers and carers working with these children may find that many of the aspects discussed below could usefully be highlighted for some of these children and made part of a programme of intervention. This is because children using wheelchairs may have a limited idea of the world, because of the height at which they are sitting and also their restricted movement. Their ability to devise routes may be affected by this. It may help them if their attention is drawn to objects and landmarks above and below them and to those in the distance.

Children with a visual impairment

Clearly, the orientation of children with a severe visual impairment is going to be seriously affected. Hill (1971) describes the use of vision in orientation as giving the ability 'to experience, stabilize, control and monitor an ever changing environment'.

For some blind children, the world does not exist beyond their arm's length in any type of coherent unity. What is out there can seem a vast uncharted space, which they are unable to order or organize. These children have poor spatial awareness skills and have a difficult time in learning how to travel. Marie was one such pupil. She was 7 years old, of near average ability, with a severe visual impairment. Although Marie had been at her residential school for two terms and had a little mobility education, she was still totally disoriented in her four-bedded dormitory. When she was on her bed, she had no mental map of the room at all. Marie was unable to get from her bed to the door, or to the cupboard where her own personal things were kept. The only clues that Marie could use were auditory and it was only by following the sound of other children that she could move around at all.

Another example of the lack of understanding about space in some children was clearly demonstrated to the writer on a visit to a school. Asked for directions as to how to get to a certain classroom, a boy with a visual impairment and with additional moderate learning difficulties said, 'If you hold on to that handrail and walk, Mrs D's classroom will come to you'. He described the negotiating of space in the terms of his own movements and he knew that if he stood in a specific place and walked, somehow he got to where he wanted to be. It is hard to imagine what his idea of reality was.

Even young people in their teens can demonstrate severe difficulties with understanding very basic concepts. A colleague described one young man, David, who appeared unable to understand the structure of buildings. David did not seem to appreciate that the second floor of a building was higher than the ground floor and that it was dangerous to climb out of the window! Colleagues used models to try and explain the concept. Eventually, the two of them climbed up a ladder on the outside of the building and felt the window that David had been climbing out of. This, the mobility specialist said, had helped, but he felt that David never really understood the concept of height.

A study undertaken by Bigelow (1991) also demonstrated the difficulties which some children who are severely visually impaired experience in understanding space. Bigelow met with blind children in their homes and asked them about the location of the rooms in their houses. Placing the children in their sitting rooms, he asked them to point to other rooms in the house. At 8 years old the blind children were able to do this for rooms on the same floor. However, many were unable to point correctly to rooms on the floor above, although sighted children were able to do this at 4 years old. The blind children who could not point directly to the location of the rooms pointed to the routes they would take to get to the room.

The child with low vision

Children with low vision also have difficulties with body and spatial concepts. Cratty and Sams (1968) administered their Body Image Test to a group of 18 blind children and 73 children who were classified as partially sighted. Interestingly, although the researchers expressed caution about the results, many of the children who were partially sighted did less well than the blind children. Cratty and Sams felt that this was probably due to the fact that the former received little specific teaching. Their study showed that it is dangerous to assume that the children with low vision have a full understanding of spatial concepts. Children with obscured vision, or who have field defects such as tunnel vision, may develop a distorted view of the environment and will need specific strategies to overcome their difficulties.

APPROACHES TO TEACHING ORIENTATION

Many specialists suggest that the basis of orientation for children with visual impairments is the children's understanding of themselves and that programmes for the development of body concepts are crucial for future orientation. Discussing the effects of a visual impairment, Cratty (1971) said:

> If the sightless child does not know the nature of the space he occupies, the manner in which he can move and the names given to his body and its parts, it is unrealistic to expect him to function in space. It is similarly unrealistic to expect a blind child, in the absence of efficient space organizers (the eyes) afforded the sighted, to organize space and to learn about space without a thorough and systematic effort made to educate him about the dimensions of himself and of his world.

The general feeling is that if youngsters lack adequate body image, they will not understand the relationship of themselves to space or other objects within it.

A different point of view has recently been put forward. Morsley *et al.* (1991) found no relationship between the 'adequacy of body image and the children's spatial and geographical skills'. The authors found that some children with a poor body image had good spatial skills and suggested that instruction for the blind child should concentrate more on alternative methods for improving large-scale space understanding, instead of concentrating on, as now, these 'close to body' skills. The authors argue that probably the most crucial factor in understanding space is direct experience of that space. The importance of direct experience is generally recognized in the literature although most programmes have suggested that a developed body image was a prerequisite of good spatial skills. One of the primary aims of all early intervention programmes is to get the infants moving as early as possible. It is good to know, however, that what mobility specialists have always felt about encouraging movement across space is now substantiated by research. Mobility teachers, working with children, have mostly taken a holistic approach. The development of body concepts has for almost all children been only part of a mobility programme. Encouraging the development of these concepts has been not so much for the orientation side of mobility as for the actual negotiation of the body through space. Children do need an understanding of the body parts, how they relate to each other and the different ways in which they move, for example, the hips move in a certain way for walking, while the hands move in a different way to manipulate objects. This understanding, the writer believes, is crucial and is one way in which children can be helped to develop good posture and other mobility skills, such as being able to walk without veering, an important skill in orientation. A knowledge of body parts is also useful for understanding instructions, for example 'the wall is waist high' and so on.

Beginning a programme

The programme should start very early in the children's lives and should not be a formal programme. The main emphasis will be on encouraging the children to be curious about the world around them and motivating them to move. Much of this motivation will depend on the attitude of the parents and of others around the youngsters. As I said in Chapter 2, there can be a tendency for carers of young children with special needs to bring the world to them rather than encourage the children to go out and explore the world for themselves. Frequently, the children are sat on rugs, in playpens or in baby chairs and are surrounded by toys. They have no reason to move. This is very natural, as parents' and other carers' first instincts will be to stimulate the children and to get them involved in activities as soon as possible, well before the children are able to crawl or walk. The main aim should be to get the children moving.

The orientation within the home will come naturally if children's natural curiosity is developed. They will want to go and find where Mother is or discover what is making the funny noise that they can hear. Young children will soon learn all the sounds associated with the kitchen and the particular water sounds of the bathroom. They will then use the sounds themselves to find their way to these rooms. The adults around the children can reinforce the children's exploration and learning through appropriate use of language which describes what the children are experiencing.

Stairs can be a source of worry to the family, who will often discourage the child with special needs from attempting these. Clearly a child's safety is paramount, but as children without special needs must learn to cope with bumps and falls, so must the children we are supporting. Although we must ensure that they do not come to any serious harm, it is not helpful if they are prevented from experiencing minor scrapes. During the child's first experiences with stairs, parents and carers will want to be close by. But the children will develop their own strategies for getting up and down stairs and will soon be able to manage them confidently.

Hopefully, the children, once they are walking, will be able to begin exploring outside, finding out what grass feels and sounds like to walk on, discovering what puddles are and beginning to identify the various noises that are heard. It can be an exciting and challenging time for the children and a rewarding time for parents. These experiences will set the basis for the more formal orientation programme, which will probably begin with the learning of some easy routes.

Routes

Although the children will, hopefully, have had a wealth of experiences within the environment before they enter school and will have worked on some informal route learning, the first formal teaching of routes will probably take place during their school years. In a school for visually impaired children, the teaching of the first, easy routes will be recognized as one of the first objectives for the children. Teachers of the children in the reception class will know from long experience which routes are both straightforward to learn and useful for the children. With the advice and support of the mobility specialist of the school, the teacher or non-teaching assistant will be able to teach the route and ensure that the children get plenty of opportunities to practise the route in meaningful situations. In special schools for children with other disabilities or in mainstream schools, this early route learning may not take place. Consideration of the environment and the children's immediate needs should lead to a decision on which route to teach first. The first route taught would possibly be from the classroom to the toilet. This will depend, however, on what the child would be required to execute to complete the route successfully. The route should not incorporate too many changes of direction and should not require the children to walk across open spaces, such as a hall. In addition, the route should be short enough to complete in a few minutes.

For most children, teaching the route should be done in stages, so that they can become confident in each part before adding another section. It is also important to build in some security landmarks outside the actual route. For example, the area at the far side of the toilet should be examined. The children, if they find themselves in this area, will know that they have gone too far and that they need to retrace their steps. It is important that both staff and children realize the differences between landmarks, that is, objects or sounds which are always present, and clues, which may be transient. They may not, for example, be able to rely on always hearing the typewriter to know that they are near the office, but it is an additional clue if they do which will confirm their whereabouts. As the children make progress with their mobility skills and their understanding of their orientation, additional routes can be introduced. These are likely to become increasingly complex.

Extended routes

The routes that the children need to learn will become longer in distance and include more numerous changes of direction. Both these factors will mean a heavier load on the children's memories. Not only will they have to remember the route for a longer time period, but they will also have more instructions to remember. The children may use orientation aids, in the form of maps or verbal routes and these are discussed later in this chapter. However, for a route that is used regularly, the children will probably rely on their memories. Each route will consist of a series of instructions which indicate landmarks and changes of direction. Although the children will learn their routes through this linear method, it is helpful if they can develop an integrated mental map of a whole area, rather than a set of self-contained, unrelated paths. One girl of 11 years of age was unable to do this. She was able to execute a number of fairly complex routes, but because she could not relate these to one another, she could only walk them if she went to the beginning point of each one. This contrasts with another pupil of the same age who could criss-cross the various routes she knew and who understood the relationship of one route to another.

One exercise to determine whether the pupils understand how to execute routes is to see if they can follow directions to unfamiliar areas of the school. If the pupils are used to travelling outside, they can be asked to follow directions for a simple route, such as walking round a block in an area which may be unknown but is not difficult. The adult will be near in case of difficulty. An exercise to determine if a route or area has been sufficiently understood is to ask the child or young person to do what is known as a 'drop off'. This is where the pupils are taken to one part of a route and asked to identify where they are and to complete the route. (The accompanying adult will take the pupil to the drop-off point by a different route from the one that is known by the pupil.)

The other aspects of an orientation programme are now discussed.

Preventing fear

The majority of children will fear moving in an unfamiliar environment. Some of this fear may have been assimilated from parents who worried about the children hurting themselves. Morsley *et al.* (1991) found that children whose parents encouraged them in free movement became spatially competent. Children whose parents were over-protective or did not understand the need for movement could arrive at school age very disadvantaged. The authors state:

'The children fear becoming lost, they fear bumping into objects and people; and if this problem is not tackled they are likely to spend much time rocking on the spot learning little of their surroundings, while their contemporaries play around them.'

Some children, it has to be said, do not appear to have any concerns about moving in familiar or unfamiliar places. This may be due to a natural sense of adventure, but perhaps it is more likely to be because they are unaware of the inherent dangers. If they have never been allowed to come across the unexpected and if their path has always been made smooth and clear, they may not realize that there are dangers. The balance must be found between giving the children a secure environment in which to learn, and giving them opportunities for risk-taking and problem-solving. If pupils are expected to use problem-solving strategies and re-orient themselves when lost and are not too quickly rescued, they will develop self-reliance. A 4-year-old (sighted or blind) can be genuinely terrified in a minute or two if they feel alone or lost. However, given verbal reassurance, even a young child can learn that they have skills which can be used to discover where they are.

Language

When giving information and directions to children, it is essential to avoid such vague terms as 'over there', 'this way', 'over here', and 'that way'. These terms have no real meaning for children without sight and they are unable to see the gestures which help to explain the directions. The children need language which is exact in order to make sense of any instructions. The actual words used will depend on the children's own understanding of spatial words. The use of 'right' and 'left' will be appropriate for some, while others may understand the positional concepts of 'front' or 'back', for example of the classroom. The requirement to be exact with any language that is used has already been mentioned. The word 'right' must not be used in any other context than in a lateral or directional sense. It must not be used to denote the correctness of any action or movement.

Patterns in the environment

Another problem for many children with special needs is a lack of real understanding of the geometrical patterns found in the physical environment. Although they may be able to describe, verbally, a definition of a square, rectangle, or triangle, they are often unable to explain how many turns they would physically need to make to walk the pattern. In addition, they may be unable to understand the shape of a corner. All this indicates an urgent need for additional training alongside programmes in cane travel (Suterko, 1972). Children with learning difficulties may have similar problems, and these pupils can be helped to understand the patterns in the environment through specific programmes. The difficulties they experience also re-enforce the need for cross-curricular work as discussed in Chapter 3.

Understanding the environment demands an understanding of a wide variety of concepts, discussed here.

Spatial concepts

Spatial language is used continually in everyday life. Here are a number of sentences which demonstrate how important spatial language is.

The door is on the left. The cellar is underneath us. You are standing between the table and the chair. The spoon is on top of your plate, and your spoon is in the mug.

Garry and Ascarelli (1969) found that many children with visual impairments could not identify the top, bottom, left, right and back of objects. They found that the children knew the words and could use these appropriately, but could not relate them to real objects. This is probably also true of many children with learning difficulties. If it is, it highlights the need for careful assessment in practical situations and for some in-depth intervention programmes to be initiated.

Environmental concepts

There is an enormous number of environmental concepts which the children need to understand in order to travel successfully. It would be impossible to include a full list in this book, which in itself gives some idea of the size of the problem. However, these concepts can be grouped into the different categories which are listed below.

Buildings: Structure and shape, walls (both the inside and outside), roof and ceiling, windows, corners (inside and outside), floors on different heights, cupboards, radiators, stairs, doors.

Many of these can be subdivided into other concepts. For example, the concept of door includes doors that are pushed and pulled, swing doors and revolving doors. Each of these is negotiated differently and should be taught under the extended mobility skills programme. However, the individual concept of doors needs to be understood if a route is to be negotiated safely and efficiently.

Pavements: Materials used (asphalt, paving, pebbles, cobbles, grass), verges, driveways (camber and lowered kerbs), trees, lamp-posts, bus stops, bus shelters, letter box, telephone box, hedges, fences, walls, house numbering systems (odd and even). Rural situations will include other concepts.

Roads and traffic flows: Roads, streets, avenues, minor and major roads, cross-roads, T-junctions, intersections, cul-de-sacs, round-abouts, driving conventions, road crossings including pelican, zebra and traffic lights.

If children are to reach more complex aspects of mobility and orientation, they need to understand how road systems are structured. Even if it is unlikely that they will reach the point when they travel independently, knowledge of these concepts will add to their overall understanding of the world in which they live.

Tooze (1981) describes her system of teaching the knowledge needed about roads. The children, either individually or in small groups, can be taken to a quiet road where they can discover all the exciting things about it.

- The inner boundary of the pavement, the inner shoreline, fences, hedges, walls (both low and high), driveways, where they go to.
- The outer shoreline, the outer boundary of the pavements. This is the kerb and examination of this will obviously take place only on a quiet road.
- The things on the pavements, trees, lamp-posts, letter boxes.
- Different types of pavement surfaces.
- Different types of roads, crescent-shaped, cul-de-sacs.

When roads are being explored may be the time to introduce the more formal terminology used in mobility. However, it is for the teacher to decide when is the appropriate time. The terminology includes terms such as inner shoreline, outer shoreline and so on (Figure 5.1).

Direction taking

There needs to be some way of indicating direction and there are two usual ways of doing this. The first is to use the clock face. The children are always told that they are facing 12 o'clock and directions given from this starting point: 'Turn to three o'clock', 'Walk to eight o'clock'. These directions are very clear to children, and until

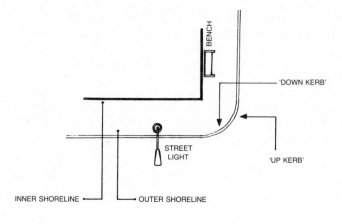

Figure 5.1

recently were very widely used. However, nowadays, fewer children are aware of the clock face. Now that digital watches are more commonly used, the clock face is not such a natural part of a child's experience. Even blind children who were used to being aware of the clock face graphic through using Braille watches are now using talking clocks. There is no reason why the clock face should not still be used, but it does mean that teachers need to ensure that children really are secure in their understanding of the clock face, before they attempt to use it for direction finding.

The second way of finding direction is through the use of compass directions. Tooze suggests the use of compass directions for explaining road layouts. 'This road runs north to south and we are on the south-west corner of the intersection.' 'Find your way to the eastern corner of the building.' This is a very useful way for explaining directions and for the children's use of maps but, again, children need to be secure in their understanding of a compass before it can be used in orientation. This is yet another cross-curricular issue and the study of geography can support the work done by the mobility specialist.

Distance

Distance is another difficulty. For sighted people, their understanding of distance comes through their vision and they relate objects in space to each other and to themselves very easily. In addition, they will have the same concept of distance as another sighted person. For children who do not see, or who do not see well, understanding distance is a difficult concept. They will build up their concepts of distance through the number of steps taken, or the time it takes to reach their destination. This will clearly be an individual perspective. We all have different stride lengths and walk at different speeds. To walk along a corridor may take one child 40 steps and take another only 20. To walk across a school campus may take one child five minutes whereas another child may take 15 minutes. Children may describe a destination as 'a long way', but this will be relative to themselves. With experience they may learn what walking 50 yards feels like, and will be able to relate it to walking 100 yards. But this will be because of the time it takes them to do it.

Their understanding of exact distance can be helped through walking with a trundle wheel. This is a wooden wheel, which takes a specific distance, for instance a metre, to do one revolution. There is a ratchet on the wheel and so a click occurs as the wheel is moved. The pupils hold on to the long handle, and count the clicks as they walk. In this way they can measure distances and begin to talk accurately about specific distances. This activity can also be related to the time taken to reach a destination. Using a stopwatch, children can time how long it takes them to walk 20 metres, 50 metres and so on. This is the sort of activity which forms part of a programme in mathematics for all children and it is especially valuable to children who do not see well. However, sighted children are able to relate these activities to the information received through their vision. Children with visual impairments will need to have this activity repeated many times if they are to understand fully the concepts involved. If these activities can be related to the children's own interests and activities, so much the better. A mobility teacher describes one such example.

> One of the best mobility lessons I ever taught was taking one of my students who was an avid baseball fan to a baseball diamond. He had listened to baseball games for years, but had never been on a baseball diamond. We ran around the bases and investigated the various dimensions of the diamond, and we walked from home base to the outer field fence. After that experience, he could better understand the concepts of what the broadcaster on the radio was talking about. This illustration again points out that the real world is the best place for real learning to take place. (Webster, 1977)

Position of things in space

Here are some suggestions for assessing the children's understanding of the relative relationship of objects and teaching children about the position of things.

1 Have the children face a chair. When they turn right, ask them to point out where the chair is now. Let them feel that the chair is now on their left. When facing the chair, and making a left turn, let them feel the chair on the right. Again facing the chair, have them make a 180° turn and point out where the chair is now. Let them find the chair behind them.
2 Have the children face a table. Ask them to turn right. Explain that the table is on the left. If the children walk forward, the position of the table changes again and becomes behind and to the left. If the children then make a 180° turn, the table becomes in front and to the right.

This is a very simple concept, but some blind children are very slow in understanding it. They do not see the changes in positions of objects in relation to themselves as they turn.

Examples of other activities which would encourage and develop this understanding would be:
3 Put the front of your body (and left, right, and back) against the wall. Point the front of you towards the sound of the radio. Move your body so the sound of the radio is on your left, right, and back. Stand so that you are by the left of the chair.

The instructions can get more complex and include more objects and more concepts, such as: Which is farther from (closer to) the kitchen stove, the refrigerator or the table? Place the chair in front of the window, and stand behind it.

Room familiarization procedures

Orientation and mobility specialists know from experience that each child must explore a room or a new area at his or her own learning rate. One child might go around the room and the walls and learn the whereabouts of everything in the room in a quarter of an hour; another child may take an hour and another child may take several weeks to become really confident. It is unfortunately not unusual for blind pupils to sit in a classroom for a year and know little about the contents of the room except where the door and their own seats are. Somehow it is assumed that the blind child will come to this knowledge without any specific teaching or intervention.

Fully sighted people are able to get a detailed knowledge of a room through a split-second glance. Children who are visually impaired have no such immediate power. Contrary to some public opinion, they have no sixth sense by which they can organize the contents of a room when entering the door. They do use their other senses, but the whole process takes far more time. After investigating all the possible relationships between the door, the four walls, the objects in the room, and the open spaces, the children must fit these together and devise a mental plan of the room. This plan must be remembered.

There are three methods that mobility specialists use to familiarize students to a room, as follows.

The perimeter method

1 Using the door as a starting point, the child walks around the room trailing the walls, until the entrance is reached once again.
2 Explain the make-up of each wall, for example, 'The wall to the left of the door (or north wall) has two windows, a bookcase and so on. The teacher's desk sits next to the wall opposite the door (or south wall).'
3 Talk to the child as she or he walks round the room trailing the walls. Describe the objects in the room and their strategic position.
4 Have the child walk around the room clockwise and anti-clockwise back to the starting point at the door until the child appears confident.
5 Back at the door, and with the child facing the room, have the child point to and describe the position of objects in the room. This is a good check to see if the child has developed a good mental map of the room.

Door–object method

1 Use the door as the starting point and major point of reference.
2 Have the child move from the door to the objects in the room (the seat in the classroom, the teacher's desk, the bookshelves, the windows, etc.) and then from each object back to the door. This will help the child build a map of the room by using the muscle memory (kinaesthetic sense).
3 When the child can locate the various objects in the room and then relocate the door, she or he is oriented.

Criss-cross method

1 Have the child walk across the room and back in both directions until she or he has covered the entire area of the room.
2 Relate the compass direction as she or he walks.
3 Point out the objects in the path of the child.

It no longer matters, then, at what starting point in the area the child is. At every point in the room, the network of objects will be clear. It will make no difference at what position the blind child is, for everything else in the room will be known.

Whichever method is used, and probably a combination of all three will be, it is important to remember that children with severe visual impairments have another disadvantage in this process. They will not notice changes in the make-up of the room, unless they have direct contact with the change, or unless someone informs them of the change.

The procedures for room familiarization have been described in detail, as the stages involved can suggest ways in which skills can be broken down, the different approaches that can be used and can also be a basis for teaching many of the other orientation tasks. The teaching of a shopping area or a railway station will include examining the perimeter and then the internal layout and a combination of the procedures for a room can, with some adaptation, fit the individual location being used.

The use of models and maps in orientation

Before discussing the role of models and maps in orientation, it is necessary to highlight the inherent difficulties for severely visually impaired people in using the tactual sense for obtaining information. It is very difficult for blind children to interpret representations in maps or models as these, initially, have little connection with the children's real life experiences. It is important that blind students are trained in the use of scanning, searching and synthesizing techniques before they are expected to use maps. Best (1992) describes the process of developing tactual skills in children. He suggests that:

> children should be taken through a sequence of exercises which start by using real three-dimensional objects. From these, the children should be exposed to raised tactile forms on paper and plastic sheets. These will not be representations of objects, which are very difficult for the blind person to understand, but abstract shapes and textures which the children can sort, match and identify.

Best also points out that tactile representations of drawings are rarely of use to blind children and gives the following example:

> A line drawing of a tree, consisting of two parallel lines for the trunk and an irregular circular top for the foliage, bears no relationship to a child's experience of the texture, shape and sound of a tree. It is so far removed from this experience as to be a separate concept.

The child has to be taught that these lines, felt through the fingers, represent a tree, as, for the child who has been born without sight, there is no real connection between the two experiences: that of feeling a tree and that of feeling the drawing.

Even three-dimensional representations are difficult for the children with severe visual impairments to understand. An example of this is the different experiences the children have of real and model cars. They know the experience of sitting in a car and indeed will describe a car in terms of the feel of the seats, the way the windows work and so on. A model car which fits into the palm of their hands and which they can push along the floor is not the same experience at all. The children may call both the real and the model 'cars' but the two experiences do not really relate. With these difficulties in mind, pre-training in the use of both models and maps is essential. There is benefit in pursuing this training as models and maps can help to give the child further information about the environment. The teaching will also be done by other staff who use maps, diagrams and models within a subject area and the methods of teaching used by all must be the same.

> Map making and the use of maps to follow routes are two activities that form an important part of orientation training. By this means the layout of the environment can be contracted to a representation small enough to be felt within the palm of the hands. Thus a blind person is enabled to appreciate the pattern of his immediate environment and the relationship between different objects within it.   (Tooze, 1981)

Verbal maps

The easiest way to give information about how to cross the environment is through a verbal route map. This consists of a series of instructions, which indicate landmarks, clues, changes of direction which need to be made, roads to be crossed and so on. Verbal maps are useful for either indoor or outdoor environments. Examples of the instructions that might be used are:

(1a) Go straight ahead to the end of the corridor.
(1b) Turn left, through swing doors, down a flight of steps, then straight ahead until the end of the corridor is reached.
(2a) Walk along the main road, crossing two minor roads, until the T-junction.
(2b) Turn left, locate and negotiate audible crossing, and cross.

These routes can be reproduced on cassette, in which case the travellers carry small tape recorders and play each instruction as it becomes necessary. Alternatively, the routes can be reproduced in written form, either large print or Braille, and the travellers read the instructions as required. The route can, of course, be memorized. However, this is really only suitable for a route that is used frequently as otherwise it is not really practical. Not only must the travellers be concentrating on the information received through the cane and paying attention to the information that is being received through the other senses, they must also be prepared to meet the unexpected. If they are having to remember a route as well, trying to identify exactly on which part of it they are, the mental effort can be very fatiguing.

There are certain guidelines which need to be considered when devising a verbal route. Routes really need to be devised with an individual in mind. Children and young people will differ in how much information they can take in and remember at any one time. The bits of information may have to be varied for different travellers. Some will prefer to have a large bit of information which, if they are able to remember it, means they can travel further without the need to stop to read the directions or play the cassette. Other young people will find remembering the information difficult. They would probably prefer to have shorter instructions, even if this means frequent stops to obtain the next stage of the route. If routes are devised for individuals the instructions can have built into them safeguards against any deficiencies of the traveller. For instance, some children may have a tendency to veer to the left. If this is so, the route can include instructions such as 'If you meet the grass you have veered to the left. Find the paving on your right.' One important principle that needs to be remembered is that the route instruction must include somewhere safe to stop each time the traveller needs to obtain the next stage of information. An instruction such as 'Find the stairs down, stop' leaves the traveller at the top of a flight of stairs, which is a very vulnerable place to stand. Finally, remember that a route map which takes a traveller from A to B will not be any use in taking them from B to A. Each left turn will be a right turn on the return journey and some landmarks will not be met at the same time as they were on the outward journey. There will need to be two routes, one for the outward and one for the return journey.

The design and use of models

The difficulty for children and young people with severe visual impairments of relating models to their experiences of the real world has already been described. It requires a great deal of experience to translate moving a finger a few centimetres within a model to moving the body several yards in the real environment. However, models can be a useful part of the varied strategies for teaching and re-enforcing the orientation of the pupils. They can be made out of a variety of materials, but the best way is probably to use bricks, particularly those that interlock, such as Lego. Bricks can be used to make models of different sizes to suit the requirements of the individual situation and which are strong enough to withstand the handling they will receive. They are also useful for the children to use to make their own models. It is important that models are large enough to allow the children to manipulate their fingers within them.

Models can be used in several ways, one of which is to reinforce their understanding of an environment. Once the child has learnt several routes within the school, for example from the classroom to the hall and from the classroom to the cloakroom, they can be shown these routes on a model. The model can also be used to demonstrate the relation between the three locations. In addition, large areas such as a playground can be shown, preferably after the child has made a preliminary exploration. If these procedures are followed, the experience gained may lead to them being able to absorb useful information from models of areas or buildings which they have never seen. However, being able to make this generalization may take several years with some pupils.

The use of maps

Tactile maps are often used to familiarize travellers who have a visual impairment with an area, such as a town centre. They are used to supplement other route learning strategies. Spencer *et al.* (1977) point out, however, that until recently little was known about how maps contributed to the person's understanding of the spatial structure of an environment, and they report on two experiments. The first was to compare the use of diagrams between sighted and visually impaired children. The groups of children, which consisted of 32 sighted children, 15 who were totally blind and 15 children who had the use of residual vision, were presented with diagrams consisting of a display of symbols. The children were allowed to examine each display until they were confident that they had learnt it. The display was then covered and the children were asked to reproduce it, using identical symbols.

The children with visual impairments did well in the study and could remember and reproduce the configuration of symbols. In fact some of the blind children out-performed the sighted children of the same age. It appeared that children who used a strategy which involved feeling the relation of the symbols to each other as well as to the outside perimeter did better than those who used a less organized strategy.

The researchers carried out a further study. A group of visually impaired children from 5 to 12 years of age were asked to learn about an environment either by directly exploring that environment or by being allowed to examine a tactile map. The particular environment used consisted of a number of toys arranged randomly in a large hall. The tactile maps were constructed by the thermoform method, a technique for producing tactile maps and Braille.

Ungar *et al.* (1993) reported that both blind and partially sighted children were able to understand and use the maps. Interestingly they found that blind children learnt the environment more accurately from the map than from direct exploration. These results certainly suggest that the use of maps can have a critical part to play in the teaching and learning about the environment, although children will make most progress if a wide variety of strategies are used. It is important, of course, to remember that even if their understanding of an environment is helped through a tactile map, the skill of transferring this knowledge to the real environment will need practice.

As has been said, in order to obtain information through the fingers the information has to be learnt sequentially, rather than in a global fashion as sighted people do. Reading tactile maps requires a number of successive hand movements and to integrate the information received through these movements places a heavy load on the cognitive processes of the children and young people. It also places a heavy load on the memory.

The making of maps

It is useful to describe the principles of map making, a few of the methods that can be used to make maps and some of the uses which can be made of them by parents and teachers. When deciding whether a map will be useful and how it should be designed, consider the following questions:

1 *What information is actually needed on the map?* There is always a danger of including too much extraneous information. This clutters the feel of the map for the pupils and may hinder their access to the information. There is often a danger when sighted people are making maps to make them visually interesting or aesthetic. This temptation must be resisted. Maps which look dull and plain to the sighted person may be the most easily discriminated and are therefore the most useful for the tactual reader. The amount of information that pupils absorb from one map will vary with the individual's tactual ability and the previous experience he or she has had with maps and diagrams. It may be necessary to make two or even more maps of the same road-crossing, street or shopping area, in order to make the information accessible.

2 *How is the labelling on the map to be managed?* Brailled text takes far more room than print text and too many words on the map may confuse the reader. It may be necessary to provide a key to the labelling and attach the additional information on a separate sheet.
3 *What is the map to be used for?* Is it a specialized map for one individual and for one specific learning situation, for example a particular road intersection? The design and the materials needed to make a temporary map to suit this situation will be different from a map which is going to be used with a group of pupils or is of a constant feature, such as a shopping centre.
4 *Is the map going to be used for classroom-based work or is it expected that the pupils will carry it around with them on mobility lessons?* Will it be used outdoors? If so, the map needs to be, as far as possible, weatherproof.
5 *Can the map be altered easily?* For example, it may be a basic map of a route to be travelled and the aim may be for the pupil to add information to the map, following an exploration exercise.

The answers to these questions will provide guidelines for the making of individual maps, which will include different aspects of size, scale, texture, density, colour and detail (Bentzen, 1980).

A map can be made in a variety of ways. It can be a sheet of paper or cardboard with symbols, lines, perhaps made with string, and textures, such as sandpaper, pasta, cotton wool, stuck on. This is not likely to be a very permanent map and clearly will not conform to any of the accepted procedures for map making. Nevertheless, such a map may be an easy and useful introduction to using maps for the young child.

Another simple way of making a map is to use a sheet of plastic film which is held steady in a frame. Drawing lines on this film with a ballpoint pen will cause raised lines to be formed, which can be felt by the user. The plastic film is relatively cheap and lasts for quite a long time. One father explained the use he made of the plastic film maps:

> Now that Sarah has good orientation and map reading skills, I make the maps to show her any new area we are going to, such as the lay-out of a hotel or shopping centre or a route to a friend's house.

Maps which are needed to be more permanent can be made through two processes, the thermoform or Minolta methods. The thermoform is a machine which uses a vacuum process. The master copy is placed under a sheet of 'plastic' paper and the heat of the machine and the subsequent cooling process allows the plastic to take the shape of the master copy. Designing and making the master plans for making copies takes a long time and involves using glue, string, cardboard and so on. Making multiple copies is cheap and the quality of the different textures for ease of discrimination can be excellent. However, some specialized knowledge of map making is needed.

The Minolta is a stereo photocopying machine which uses a special paper to produce any black lines on the master in raised form. The paper is expensive and, in addition, diagrams produced in this way need to be kept simple. The markings tend to be the same height and the range of symbols is determined by those that can be produced by a pen (Best, 1992).

There are a number of established conventions in the preparation of maps. The symbols used on maps are of three main types: area, linear and point. The area symbols are used to indicate 'areas such as seas, lakes, forests and mountains on small-scale maps and buildings, grass and ponds on large-scale maps'. Linear symbols are used to show continuous features such as roads and railways. Point symbols indicate specific locations and landmarks, such as specific shops, bus stops and so on.

Further information on map making can be obtained through reading Law (1987) and Hinton (1988); the Royal National Institute for the Blind is also a useful source of information.

Technology

Various types of technology can usefully be used as part of the orientation programme. Maps and diagrams have already been mentioned. The use of computers and graphic software also has a place. It would be impossible to describe all the various types of software programs. However, one piece of equipment that has recently been devised is the Nomad and this has a particular application for orientation.

Nomad is a touch-sensitive pad, about 40 × 28 cm in size, on which raised line graphics or other pictures can be placed. The Nomad pad is connected to a computer, which is loaded with Nomad software. Information about the graphic is entered on the computer and stored in a named field. Once a graphic and a data file have been created they can be used over and over again. Information can also be added or deleted at a later stage. The information about the chart, map or diagram is programmed via the computer keyboard and is presented through a speech program, when the chosen point on the graphic is pressed.

Once created, people who are blind or visually impaired can learn independently about geography, geometry and anything involving charts, diagrams or photos, with multi-media presentation enhancing and reinforcing the learning process. It is especially useful in mobility as the geography of an area can be shown with information about the area presented aurally. It can also be used as a talking directory for buildings and campuses. Unfortunately it is rather expensive and it is unlikely that individual mobility teachers will have access to one. However, most special schools for visually impaired students will have one.

Problem-solving

Perhaps the most important skill which is needed in independent travel is problem-solving. If the pupils can recognize that they are on their intended route, identify where they are and take appropriate strategies to get themselves to where they want to be, independent travel has been achieved.

One important way to develop this skill is through the attitude taken by the mobility teacher when children deviate from an intended route. This should not be viewed as an error and children should not feel that they have made a mistake or failed. The adults should use this situation in a positive way and as an opportunity for further exploration and problem-solving. A 13-year-old girl, Jennie, was very nervous about making 'mistakes' until her teacher started saying 'That was just a little detour. A detour doesn't matter.' Soon Jennie was able to say cheerfully 'Well, I got here all right – just a little detour on the playing field'. The teachers can also make it a deliberate policy to 'change their minds'. Halfway from the science block to the gymnasium, they can say 'Let's go to the swimming pool instead. How could we do that?'

Another important aspect of the mobility specialist's work in developing problem-solving skills is to find the right balance between supporting the children and not allowing them to be frustrated or upset by the challenges offered, and offering the chance to solve the problems for themselves. The skill and experience of the mobility specialist will enable him or her to find this critical balance. Most adults, when working with children with special needs, tend to intervene too soon when children meet problems. Mobility teachers will use their knowledge of the individual pupils well, considering their maturity and the strategies they have available, and then decide how quickly to help them. Until children are old enough to be really alone, they will need the reassurance that adults will always be nearby and watching and will help in case of serious trouble.

Devising and implementing programmes of orientation for children with special needs can be great fun and very rewarding for the staff involved. Through cross-curricular activities and specific teaching objectives, the children's progress can be remarkable.

6

Mobility and orientation for children with additional disabilities

INTRODUCTION

Parents and educators of children with profound disabilities and complex difficulties have done much to improve the educational practice for all children and young people. Careful analysis of the individual strengths and problems of their pupils has improved the assessment techniques of teachers of other pupils. The continual refining of the task-analysis approach to specific objectives has fed into teaching approaches with other children. I believe that the same is true in the mobility and orientation areas. Teachers and mobility specialists involved with these children have had to take an in-depth look at the children and their mobility needs and devise new and creative ways of helping them take the next step, for them, to independent movement and travel. The expertise that these professionals have developed and are continuing to develop will require those working in mobility with other children and young people to take a fresh look at their mobility curriculum and the teaching methods which are used. Many traditional skills will be needed, but they may not be needed or be able to be taught in the same order. Joffee and Rikhe (1991) describe pupils who could use a long cane when walking across an open space long before the skills which usually precede this had been mastered. A few mobility specialists in Britain have questioned whether it was appropriate or even correct to change the usual teaching order of skills for these children. Although some professionals may disagree, many of those who, like myself, have worked with these children feel the answer is 'yes'. The safety and success factors must be ensured and the teaching methods of long-experienced mobility specialists should be observed, but it is clear that with many of these children, tradition will not have the answer.

> For the seriously multiple-handicapped human being, mobility is the capacity to move, so that he can arrive, in his own way and within the

limits of his possibilities, at enjoyable experiences and that he will be able to withdraw from unpleasant experiences.   (Harley *et al.*, 1987)

This statement affirms the importance of developing the orientation and mobility skills of children with multiple disabilities. Harley *et al.* further suggested that these children 'can benefit from carefully programmed instruction' and that early home-based intervention with these children can be very effective. This of course presupposes the availability of mobility specialists to work within the home and to provide training for both parents and children and, until very recently, few mobility specialists have been involved with children with complex difficulties. For many of these children, mobility and orientation have received little emphasis in their daily curriculum.

Fortunately, over recent years a few mobility teachers have begun to look at the needs of these children. Rogow (1988) noted Berdell Wurzburger's early contributions to educating multi-disabled children in mobility and orientation. Rogow comments that blind children with learning difficulties who were 'barely able to walk when training began, learned to walk with independence and confidence'. She also quotes his words: 'Get them up, get them moving.' As more teachers and mobility specialists involve themselves in developing skills, particularly of orientation, the knowledge will grow and expertise on how to adapt both the programme and mobility aids will spread to all those who work with these children.

The skills in mobility and orientation are too often equated with the use of the long cane or a guide dog and totally independent travel. This is not so, and we denigrate the achievements of the children and young people, particularly those with multiple disabilities, if this point of view is taken. The mastery of any skill in mobility or orientation is an important step for these students and develops their understanding of the world around them. The child who has several disabilities who has learnt where the door of the classroom is, whether or not he or she can actually physically move to it, is mastering mobility. Children who, at whatever age, begin to move are gaining control over their bodies and their environment. It does not matter how they move, how ungainly or how awkwardly, the important thing is that they are moving. Each stage in the decreasing of dependence is an increase in independence. We cannot know when the children are small quite how far along the continuum of mastering mobility and orientation skills they will get. Many parents and teachers have been surprised at the level of independent travel which the children achieve.

Murdoch (1989) describes her experiences of teaching Donald, a 9-year-old deaf-blind boy. As Donald was very motivated to move and had always enjoyed exploration and had a long programme of informal mobility education, it was decided to assess his skills more formally. Murdoch reports: 'He showed good body awareness and body image; confident independent movement around familiar environments; the abilities to trail and to protect himself (for example shielding his face with an arm near head-height obstacles) and confident movement when guided by an adult on unfamiliar terrain.' As a result of this assessment, it was decided to introduce formal mobility techniques to Donald, including the introduction of the long cane. Murdoch goes on to describe the initial sessions: 'Donald began long-cane work by sitting on the floor and finding a plate of crisps on it. As the plate was moved further away, so Donald's own arm sweep no longer found it; sweeping with a cane, however, rapidly located the crisps. Once the principle of locating out-of-reach objects was established, we moved to negotiating a corridor full of obstacles.' After the programme had been implemented for some time, Donald was reported as requesting his cane when going out and being able to decide when and where the cane would be of use to him. The teachers felt that the next step would be to learn a route outside the school environment. At the beginning of that programme, no one could have known how well Donald would do.

The skills of mobility and orientation are crucial for these pupils and should be incorporated into the daily curriculum and routine of the children, who should also receive any specific individual teaching which they require. As these children's problems are so complex and their needs so individual, a whole-school multi-disciplinary approach is vital. In addition it will need to be recognized that, as Lessard (1989) points out, programmes of intervention for children and young people with several disabilities will need to be a long-term commitment. Mobility training for adventitiously blind children, and even for some bright children with congenital visual impairments, can be of a short duration; mobility specialists can see their input being for a limited amount of time. However, for children and adults with multiple handicaps, mobility education will need to go on for many years and may never be concluded. In this country, there is a developing practice of placing people who need long-term care in the community rather than in segregated institutions. If care in the community is to be successful and functional integration is to take place, mobility and orientation education will be essential.

A multi-disciplinary approach

This book argues for a multi-professional and cross-curricular approach to education in mobility and orientation. With children who have additional difficulties to their visual impairment or who are profoundly disabled, this is particularly important. The staff who are most intimately involved with the child must be fully involved with the mobility programme. They will know the best means of communicating with the child and they will also know what is the most motivating factor for each individual. A multi-disciplinary approach will also ensure that everyone understands the implications of the pupil's residual vision, hearing impairment or mobility aid. There must be a totally co-ordinated and consistent approach with the same language or communication system being used by every member of staff and, of course, the family. Any routes which are taught must be described in the same way by all those supporting the child. The teacher will be able to provide information on the child's cognitive development, the physiotherapist will have a particular expertise in the motor development, and the mobility specialist will be able to advise on the stages of the child's programme of mobility and orientation. All of this expertise is required and close co-operation is essential. There is a danger of tension occurring between different professionals if this co-operation does not exist. The physiotherapist may be anxious that a child walks as much as possible and the teacher may be concerned about the resulting high levels of fatigue in the child. Discussion between all those involved with the child will help to prevent these difficulties occurring.

As with mobility and orientation for other children with special needs, those with multiple disabilities will gain much from other areas of the curriculum. A programme of dance or drama, for example, will help these students develop their balance, posture, spatial awareness and co-ordination, which are all important aspects of mobility. All physical activities will support the development of mobility and orientation skills, but every area of the curriculum should be used to develop the pupil's independence.

The complex problems

The difficulties which face children with multiple disabilities are many. These difficulties also pose challenges for the adults who are working with these children. Children who are additionally disabled will be caused many problems even if the additional difficulty is relatively minor. Children who are not regarded as having a major physical disability may well have impaired abilities in maintaining their stability, co-ordinating their body movements or attaining correct posture. They may also have a lack of strength and many will have a great fear of movement. Children and young people who have learning difficulties and have an additional visual impairment, even if this is not considered severe, may have great difficulty in making sense of what they see. A careful analysis of the children's difficulties is required in order to understand exactly what is preventing progress. It may be that a child who is unable to achieve certain motor skills is having difficulty in understanding the task and it is the cognitive aspect that is preventing progress and not a physical difficulty. An example of this is the child who is able to walk, but cannot meet the objective 'walks alone across the room' because the instruction or the concept of walking across space to a destination is not understood. It may, of course, also be that the space is a frightening void and it is the child's fear that prevents him or her achieving the objective. Assessing the different levels of functioning in these children will include a consideration of all these factors.

Assessment of the children's present level of functioning

As all parents, teachers and those involved with the children will know, every programme of intervention will begin with answering the following questions: What is the child's current level of achievement? What can he or she do now? What are the child's particular strengths and difficulties?

In considering functioning in mobility and orientation, the following questions will help to compile a profile of the child:

1 Is it possible to say what clues the child uses in his or her movement within the environment; auditory, tactile, etc?
2 Is the child's ability to move impaired? How? (This may vary from a child who has a poor gait or posture to the very physically disabled child who has little motor control.)
3 Does the child show an interest in moving?
4 What appears to motivate the child to move?
5 Can the child move purposefully, such as respond to a request like 'Come to me', or move to a particular place, such as the toilet, hall or playground?
6 Does the child appear to know where he or she is; in the classroom, in the wider environment?
7 Does the child understand early route taking, for example how to move from place to place such as from door to seat, classroom to toilet? Note that a child using a wheelchair may still be able to understand how to get to different places even if he or she is

unable to move there unaided. This also applies to other non-ambulant children.

8 How well is the child able to perform within the real situation, as opposed to an artificially devised one?
9 Is the child able to communicate any need for assistance?
10 What would seem to be the next stage, developmentally, that should be encouraged?
11 How far does this next stage need to be subdivided into steps that are small enough for each individual child to achieve success? (Stone, 1992)

Clearly, for these questions to be answered fully, advice and information will be required from a number of different professionals, such as the physiotherapist and, of course, the parents. There will also be a need to refer to more detailed assessment procedures. These do need, however, to be approached with a certain amount of caution when used with children who have very complex problems and the individual nature of the child's strengths and difficulties must be the central feature of any assessment. A list of procedures which may be helpful in the assessment of these children is given in the appendices.

Motivating movement

It may be that the child has found security in stillness and that moving has proved too dangerous or too painful. Carers may also have played an unwitting part in discouraging children from moving. They may have prevented the child from moving rather than expose the child to any chance of hurting themselves. But there are safe activities that can be used to encourage the children to move. At a very basic level, the child can be rolled over during nappy changes (always watching for the safety factors and taking appropriate advice first). The 'soft play' areas which are often found in special schools are an obvious example of a safe situation to encourage movement. It is also possible to devise safe obstacle courses, in which the children can learn to move up, down, in, over, under and so on. These encourage the child to move and also encourage the development of these spatial concepts. Thomas (1991) advocates the use of a large cardboard box which keeps objects in a confined space, allows the child to feel secure in a small environment and encourages them to start extending their reach out and away from their body. Later on, it will be necessary to encourage the children to extend their movement through reaching out, upwards and sideways. This can be motivated by holding something with a well-liked sound or smell just out of reach. This is where the parents' and the teachers' expertise is crucial, because they will know which are the favourite objects for the child and be able to advise other professionals. How far these skills can be developed depends to a large extent on how mobile the child is. But even a child who is only able to roll over or move a few yards can experience a change of surface, for example, rolling from a carpet to a lino floor. The child may show a dislike of the lino floor. Great. It shows that the difference between the carpet and the lino has been discriminated and the child is demonstrating a preference. It may also motivate the child to move – away from the hard cold surface.

McInnes and Treffrey (1982) feel that the main difficulty in getting children to move is finding a reason to do so, but they list a number of activities which children with deaf-blindness have undertaken and enjoyed. These activities include horse riding, swimming, ice skating, skiing and creative and formal dancing. The authors go on to say that the base for these sophisticated activities is established in the early years and argue that every effort should be made to encourage the children to use any movement ability they have for purposeful activity. McInnes and Treffrey suggest that children should be expected to fetch and return their toys as soon as they have sufficient movement to do so. If parents and carers can find the time and the required patience, the children's orientation can be encouraged through joining in with routine movements around the house, for example fetching the milk or post, making the beds and so on. Adults working with the children should be watching for any sign that the children want to move, and then act upon it, providing any support necessary.

A developmental programme

The early training of mobility specialists gave them the skill to train adults who had lost their sight to travel independently. Specialists could confidently expect that their clients would have well-developed movement and good spatial and environmental concepts. The same is not true of children and young people, particularly of those with multiple disabilities. Any programme of mobility and orientation must be based on the children's developmental age. They may be at different stages in the various areas of development; motor, cognitive, emotional and so on.

It was also thought by mobility specialists that there were some developmental foundations which were required for mobility and orientation to be successful, including a knowledge of concepts of the body and the space surrounding it, independent locomotion, the ability to follow directions, receptive and expressive language, basic intellectual skills and emotional stability. However, some studies have suggested that these abilities and skills are not necessarily prerequisites for mobility and orientation education. For example, Gee and Goetz, cited in Gee *et al.* (1987), found that students with severe disabilities who had not achieved all these sub-skills were able to learn some specific mobility and orientation skills, including a modified trailing technique, manoeuvring around obstacles and trailing along walls. This does suggest that perhaps a fresh look needs to be taken at the traditional programme of mobility. Specialists working with these children must be encouraged to share their knowledge and experience. Nevertheless, it is important that attention is given to all areas of the mobility curriculum and that the children's movement and travel within the environment is approached in exactly the same way as children's learning in any other area of development.

An additional difficulty for some of these children was highlighted by Fraiberg (1977), who pointed out that one of the problems for children with severe visual impairments is that until they can crawl, the floor and room space cannot be mapped and understood by them, and until they can find and move towards objects they will not have the motivation and security to crawl. If there is delayed motor or cognitive development, the children may not have sufficient experience of the environment to ensure that this mapping of space takes place. Developmental programmes must include an awareness of these implications.

Communication

The heavy reliance on the use of verbal instruction and verbal feedback that is typical of traditional mobility and orientation instruction may exclude children and young adults with dual or profound disabilities (Gee *et al.*, 1987). If a mobility specialist is involved with the children, it may be necessary that they devote time to learning the particular communication system used in the school or by a particular child. The difficulty in communicating with these children has been one of the reasons why mobility specialists have not frequently been involved with them. But this difficulty is one that can be overcome and mobility specialists must devote the necessary time to learn how to communicate through the child's own system.

Objects of reference which are part of the communication system of many children with profound disabilities can be used in mobility. Joffee and Rikhe (1991) described the symbols that were used in a mobility programme for such pupils. Examples included a spoon for the cafeteria, a toilet-paper roll for the toilet and a backpack for the school bus. Teachers in Britain have developed their own objects of reference for pupils and these can and should be incorporated into the mobility programme.

Social skills

McInnes and Treffrey (1982) explain that the acquisition of social skills is important as it 'will enable him to utilise the assistance of others in order to function independently of their direction'. Social skills will mean that the children can use other people to assist them, not to think for them. The aim is to increase the children's control over the environment, which includes other people, and to begin to incorporate this control in decision-making. Education about social skills will be a main feature of the total curriculum for the children and young people and this simply needs extending into the mobility programme.

Body awareness

Massage in the physiotherapy sense can be enormously helpful and many children with multiple disabilities receive such therapy. But a different type of massage, gently stroking the skin, can be given by parents and carers to increase the children's awareness of their bodies. There are many daily activities which can provide opportunities for this type of massage. For example, when bathing the children care can be taken to 'flannel' the child all over the body, including the individual toes and fingers, the elbow, the backs of the legs and the back. These are all areas of the body of which we may not always be conscious. Take a pause in reading this. Can you feel your individual toes? Probably not, particularly if you are wearing socks or shoes. The same may apply to our backs and the tops of our heads, unless our backs are against the chair we are sitting in or we have a headache! We are aware of the parts we can see, and the parts that are in contact with something else, for example the soles of our feet with the floor. Children with complex disabilities need help in 'feeling' the parts of their bodies that they are not normally aware of. Without care being taken to help the children become aware of their body parts, especially for the children with little or no vision, the image they have of themselves will be very limited.

Early movement

Children also get to know and experience their own body by means of movement and postures. Some children will be able to respond to teachers' requests to do certain movements, but on the whole the children will need to have the adult's help in learning to move. This calls for a specific expertise on the part of the teacher and a very great trust in the teacher by the child. Having one's body manoeuvred into new movements can feel very threatening. Once the children are comfortable with having their limbs moved, more extensive movements can be tried. These will help the child's self-awareness and the realization that their bodies are separate from the rest of the world. Many schools for children with these difficulties have regular movement sessions where there is one adult helper to each child and movements are made to music and singing. This will all help the children's understanding, not only of their own bodies but also the space around them.

Thomas was the mobility officer at Rushton Hall School. This is a school for multi-disabled blind children. He took a keen interest in these particular pupils and developed strategies for developing the mobility and orientation skills of the pupils, all of whom had very complex difficulties. He pointed out (1987) that these children have a very limited awareness and understanding of the environment outside their arms' reach.

Lilli Nielson (1979), whose work with multi-disabled blind children is well known, discusses the very early movement patterns of these children. In her book *The Comprehending Hand* she says:

> When the child, lying on his stomach, is able to raise his head, he will then stretch his fingers so the hands are positioned ready to support the weight of the body. The child now not only lifts up his head, but also his shoulders and chest. This capacity to be able to use the hand and arms for support is necessary for the child to master such operations as reaching out for objects, for getting into a hands and knees position for crawling, for sitting up to guard against falling and to train the capacity to keep a proper balance when in the upright position and to be able to walk.

There have recently been many creative ideas to help children with multiple disabilities to make contact with and relate to the world, including resonance boards, tactile mats and stimulation rooms. These can be enormously helpful in motivating children to move and for introducing the very basic concepts needed for mobility and orientation. Nielson describes her work with a resonance board.

Resonance boards

> Place the infant instead in a prone position on a platform made of 4 mm veneer measuring 1.20 x 1.50 m. The platform should be raised 2–3 cm above floor level, then every movement made by the child

will not only produce a noise, but the noise will be transmitted by the veneer. By this means the sound quality of the child's activity will be reinforced, and there is a good chance that the child will be able to sense it and be inspired to make further movements. Gradually the child will understand that the sounds he hears are sounds that he is creating himself.

The child's desire to move and lift his head can be increased even more if sound-producing objects are placed under his head.

If a flat plastic plate is placed underneath the child's head, then a sound will be made at the least movement of the child.

If the plate is rubbed with the rind of an orange or powdered with vanilla sugar the child will not only receive reinforcement of the sound impressions by the movements made, but he will also receive impressions of smell and even taste, if he begins to explore his surroundings by sucking on the plate.

Many teachers now work with a resonance board and this can enhance the 'reality' of the environment for the children. Thomas explains that the resonance board also provides a platform upon which articles which are dropped or 'lost' can be found more easily through the resonant qualities of the board.

Tactile mats

As has been said, children with multiple disabilities may lack the motivation to reach out and explore the environment and their movements may be limited to random reaching, just touching things accidentally. A tactile mat can bring the environment to the children, while still giving them the sense of security which is so essential for many of them. If the children are regularly placed on a mat in the same position and place, they can begin to learn, for example, that the noise maker is on the left, the rope above them, the scouring pad on the right and the rustle of material by their feet. They can then be helped to relate their bodies in space, learn how to avoid textures they dislike and search for preferred objects. Objects and textures can of course be varied, and through careful observation teachers can learn about the likes and dislikes of the children. Tactile mats can come in many forms: a child's favourite sweatshirt on the floor, a cover over a wedge and, for hand activities, a cushion on the tray of a wheelchair.

Stimulation rooms

There are a number of environments provided within schools which can afford many opportunities for encouraging the children to move. These are rooms which have multi-sensory stimulation with a vast array of different lighting and sound systems. Most of these incorporate interactive operation: the child is rewarded for a movement or particular action with a sound or light. Although there has been a certain amount of discussion and dissension about the use of these environments (Orr, 1993; McLarty, 1993), the general consensus seems to be that, when there are specific objectives in mind, these rooms can be a useful addition to the teacher's repertoire.

Use of the other senses

Any experience of using a wheelchair or crutches while wearing simulating spectacles will demonstrate how difficult it is to concentrate on navigation, the information that is being received through the other senses and the distorted visual images. There is too much concentration needed on the task in hand, perhaps moving the wheelchair or trying to make sense of the distorted images that are seen through the spectacles, to concentrate on the orientation side of travel. Children with multiple disabilities have similar though greater difficulties. While they are, for example, trying to maintain their balance as they walk around, it may be almost impossible for them to concentrate on the sounds in the environment. Children who have learning difficulties may not realize what information these sounds can give them. The limited understanding they may have of the meaning of these sounds further compounds the difficulties. It will be helpful to provide situations where the children have to concentrate on only one thing. The child who has difficulty walking can be pushed on a small tricycle while being asked to listen to and interpret sounds. Similarly, blind children can be guided while they are learning to make use of the tactile clues that they discriminate with their feet or hands. Best (1992) describes 'hand clues', which are aids to mobility obtained through the tactile sense:

> Hand clues are any pieces of information that are obtained through the hands. They can usually be discerned through 'trailing' – the hand is held in front of and to the side of the body with the back of the hand forwards. In this way the fingers are not forced backwards if they unexpectedly hit an object. Children can be alerted to many naturally occurring hand clues. Banisters are an example. They are most helpful if they are continuous and finish at least level with the bottom step so that the end of the banisters clearly indicates the end of the steps. Door handles, dado rails, table surfaces, wall coverings and so on can all be used to help establish position and direction of movement. Hand clues can also be introduced into a setting to provide

extra support for a child. Plastic or wooden shapes can be fastened on to a child's chair, drawer and peg to make them easier to find; textured wallpaper can be added to a wall just in front of a door or near the beginning of a flight of stairs; distinctive handles can be used to help in the identification of different doors in a corridor. These extra clues need not necessarily draw attention to the blind child's special needs. For example, warning of a door in a corridor could be given by gluing several strands of nylon fishing line to the wall to form a tactile patch of vertical stripes. It will be easily felt by the child but go unnoticed by many sighted people.

The first routes

Even when children are developmentally ready to walk across space, they may not make any move to do so. When they were learning to stand, they always had the security of being in contact with some object, a piece of furniture or an adult. For children with visual and additional disabilities, the initial movement away from physical contact with a base and into space can be a very difficult and terrifying experience. This fear must be understood. Physical support must be reduced gradually and replaced by verbal support, which must again be reduced very gradually. Trailing the walls will probably be the first way to help children understand the environment, and from this they progress to walking in and across space. Even while the child is trailing, it may be necessary for the adult to hold their hand in the first instance, but the aim should be to reduce the amount of contact over a period of time. Progress to this could first be through touching the child on the shoulder every time they take a step, then every other step, and so on. Verbal contact replaces tactile contact, with the child's name being repeated or reassuring comments such as 'Good', or 'I'm here' or 'You're at the wall' being made. The aim should be for the child eventually to walk a short route without any support, either tactual or verbal. The trailing can be made more interesting and useful for orientation by putting interesting textures on the walls (at the right height for the child). Textures such as bubble paper, egg boxes and foil can motivate the child to find the next one and can be associated with certain parts of the route (Thomas, 1987). If it is possible for the child to walk barefoot on occasion, this can be helpful, not only to exercise the feet but to enable them to receive direct sensations from ground surfaces (the ground will of course have been checked for safety first).

It is important for a teacher to recognize the specific channels of perception and to understand the fragmentary nature of the information received through these channels. If this is fully understood then adults will be able to help the children make sense of the world around them. This includes hearing the clock ticking and pointing it out to the child, referring to it constantly. The adults must keep themselves 'clued up' to changes in the auditory, tactile and olfactory information that is around the children. This can be difficult to do for sighted people and it is necessary to keep the senses alert. Tom, a pupil with multiple disabilities with whom I worked, became distressed at a certain point in a corridor. Trying to discover what was upsetting him I decided it was probably the very large windows along the corridor, which gave a very different feeling to the corridors in other parts of the school. After several attempts to reassure him about the different feel of the corridor, with no success, a colleague pointed out the hum of the boiler, which could be heard in the corridor. This was not a constant sound in the corridor and my hearing had not identified it as a distinctive sound. This proved to be what was upsetting Tom. Once we had appreciated the cause of his concern, it then became a possible objective to enable him to overcome it. You do need to take time to encourage exploration. Do the children know how doors work, how toilet seats lift, how floor cushions can be moved? There can be a tendency to want to make haste too quickly. Negotiating the corridor can become too task-focused; insufficient time is spent having fun in the corridor, investigating doors, finding out who or what is behind each one. If communication between adult and the child is possible, discussion can take place on what might be met next. The following is an example of a conversation between a mobility specialist and a child with multiple disabilities.

'Whose room is this?'
'Johnson's' (that is, Mrs Johnson).
'How do you know?'
'Her noise' (typing).
'Let's go in and say Hello to her... What do we come to next?'
'Toilets.'
'How will you know when you get there?'
'Water.'

Obviously both sides of the corridor will have to be investigated in this way. After a period of trailing the walls, the child may be persuaded to leave actual contact with the wall for a few steps or moves. As confidence grows, the next stage would be to move down the corridor without touching it while being close enough to touch it if that extra bit of security is needed. The final stage will be to encourage the child to move away from the walls and to walk in the middle of the corridor. (As may be imagined, this is a much safer place to be, away from the opening of doors and the chance of people suddenly emerging.)

CHILDREN WITH DUAL SENSORY IMPAIRMENTS

Mobility and orientation with pupils who are both visually and hearing impaired present very complex problems. When considering mobility and orientation for children with visual impairments, whether or not they have additional physical or learning difficulties, the sense of hearing is used to obtain information about the environment. For children who have a hearing impairment as well as a visual impairment, some parts of the programme will necessarily be more difficult, and perhaps impossible. But there are still goals that can be achieved.

Any aid to hearing or vision that the child normally uses should be present and operational. In addition, the implications of the use of the aids should be understood by the mobility teacher. As with all areas of the children's learning, mobility and education must be part of the total developmental curriculum. Using the communication system of each child, they can be guided through a simple route. The routes chosen must be very simple and must have meaning for the child. It may be helpful to have extra tactile markers for feeling with hands or feet, whichever seems most appropriate for the child. Mackey (1988) felt that a long-cane programme could go some way to overcoming the difficulties posed by dual sensory loss and encouraging independent travel. She felt, however, that crossing roads would always be a hazard which might prove insurmountable.

PHYSICAL DISABILITIES

Students in wheelchairs and on crutches can also become more independent, but different strategies will be required. Teachers must monitor carefully the distances travelled by children whose walking causes them difficulty (Tingle, 1990). Fatigue from general mobility difficulties will quickly be reflected in a deterioration of fine motor control and general lack of concentration. Should their physical condition make the children more vulnerable, then they must be saved from potentially dangerous situations. The input of a physiotherapist should be asked for on a regular basis to advise on walking aids, callipers and so on.

Voight (1989) suggests that there are two responses to the question 'What about blind wheelchair drivers?'. The first is that it is impossible for a blind wheelchair driver to become independent, and the second is that a person with even these disabilities can become *more or less* independent. As a blind wheelchair driver himself, Voight had to improve his handling of his wheelchair and then find a suitable aid to his orientation and body protection. Voight found the sonic guide, described in Chapter 1, to be the most useful and he was able to use environmental sound and to move alongside traffic in the same way as a long-cane user. He wrote: 'Thus I learnt to use traffic, parked cars near the pavement, trees and lamp-posts as an outer shore line and hedges, fences and walls as an inner shoreline.' Voight stated that his only major difficulty was the fact that the sonic guide does not detect kerbs or stairs going down, but he advised everybody who is blind and a wheelchair driver to try out mobility training. Although Voight is clearly a determined and highly motivated individual, his achievements perhaps suggest that we restrict the experiences offered to our children by the limits of our own expectations.

It is, of course, essential that the pupil is thoroughly comfortable with the equipment that is being used before being asked to concentrate on orientation. The need for a feeling of security will probably be even greater than for the fully ambulant visually impaired pupil.

Rogow (1988) suggests the following stages for pupils who are in wheelchairs:

- Trail a clear path.
- Locate doorways.
- Detect obstacles.
- Avoid obstacles.
- Make turns.
- Open simple doors.
- Transfer from the wheelchair to another chair independently.

The use of bare feet for ambulant children has already been suggested. For many wheelchair-bound children, too, it may be possible to allow them to travel with bare feet, feeling different textures placed on the walls (placed, of course, at a suitable height). This can make travel far more interesting than simply being pushed from place to place in a void.

Moving a child about in a wheelchair can be either a positive activity for the child or a negative one. Which of these it is depends on the attitude of the carers and their understanding of the implications of each situation and each journey.

A situation involving a girl called Ruth is an example of this. Ruth was a blind girl of 7 who was also very physically disabled and confined to a wheelchair. She was sitting with a group of children at a table. Because of a change of activity, it was necessary to move

Ruth to sit on the other side of the table next to Graham. As the classroom was crowded and a lot of the children were in wheel-chairs, it was easier to take Ruth around the outside of the class-room. The 'route' is shown in Figure 6.1. Ruth, having spent several minutes 'travelling', was very surprised to find herself next to Graham, only a foot or so away from where she had been sitting previously.

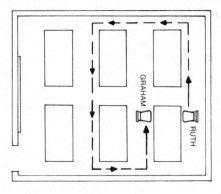

Figure 6.1

If the person who had been taking Ruth around the classroom had explained what was happening and what route was being taken, Ruth's orientation would have been improved and extended. As it was, the experience left her very confused. It is likely that this situation is repeated in many classrooms. Without the actual physi-cal movement of the body, orientation is difficult for children with visual impairments and additional physical disabilities, but some of the pupils become extremely well-oriented to their surroundings.

Guidelines for moving children in wheelchairs

There are likely to be a number of adults involved with these chil-dren in schools and it is important that everyone who is involved with taking children in wheelchairs is aware of the techniques, not only of pushing wheelchairs, but also of the ways in which to make the children's travel a comfortable and meaningful experience.

For example, Thomas (1987) points out that when ambulant children are being taken from place to place, they are often held by the hand which gives a secure feeling and also builds up relation-ships between them and the adults, whereas children in wheelchairs have little contact with the person pushing them. Placing a hand on the children's shoulders while they are being pushed can be very reassuring. This is particularly important for the children who have visual impairments, but the same principle also holds good for all the children. Another point to be remembered is that because of the different height of children in wheelchairs and of the adults pushing them, together with the fact that the children are facing away from the adults, the children may not hear the adults talking to them. It is necessary for the adult to lean forward towards the children and ensure that they can hear the adult's voice.

Any traveller in a wheelchair being pushed by another person can find it an uncomfortable experience. Children in wheelchairs may, in addition, feel very threatened and vulnerable as they are the ones in front and may be being pushed along at what may seem to them a frightening speed. It can be disturbing if the wheelchair is pushed into a door in order to open or close it. This may seem a tempting thing to do for the adult, who may well be in a hurry, but it is frightening for the children. If it is possible, they should be involved with the opening and closing of doors. The adult will feel very protected behind the wheelchair, but must remember the feeling of vulnerability of the children. It may be tempting, too, to cut corners and to move the wheelchair in a rather swinging fashion. This, too, can be frightening for the children, and in addition it does nothing to help their orientation. Corners in corridors which have 90° turns should be taken at 90°.

Rogow (1988) describes the adaptations to the mobility programme which were made for a girl with a visual impairment who also used crutches. When being guided, instead of holding on to the guide's arm, Katie was taught to follow the sound of the guide's voice and footsteps. Information was given to her on turns to be made, changes in direction, obstacles in the path and slopes up or down. Instead of the normal trailing procedure, Katie took several steps with her crutches and then used one of them to check that she was still close to the wall. The routes chosen and devised for her were those which allowed her to remain in contact with a wall or other landmark as much as possible. Katie was able to identify doorways and openings along walls and by using one of her crutches to help her balance, she was able to use the other to locate landmarks on either side of her.

Children who are more mobile – those who can crawl or walk – can be exposed to a large number of surfaces. In the summer they can move on grass or sand, while the inside environment can provide many different tactile experiences, such as the feel of short- and deep-pile carpets, linoleum and so on. Children who are being pushed around in wheelchairs should also be told about the different surfaces and encouraged to listen to the differences in sound that the wheelchair makes as it travels over them.

The use of the cane and other aids

I have already mentioned that the long cane is usually associated with a highly sophisticated level of mobility. But many children with additional difficulties can find using the cane and particularly pre-canes helpful. As it is unlikely that the child or young person will be using the cane independently in complex situations, such as busy roads or shopping centres, it is not necessary or desirable to be over-concerned about achieving the techniques described in Chapter 4, although this section of the book should be used when the child begins to use the cane. Teachers, parents and others must adapt the techniques to suit the individual child. For example, the cane does not have to be moved in the correct arc. It can simply be pushed in front of them by the child. This will give the child warning of obstacles or drops and may enable them to have a much freer and relaxed movement. But the cane is not the only thing that can be used. Pushing toys such as carts and tricycles that can be sat on can also have a place, as can anything that prevents the child from bumping into things, although the cane does have several advantages over such toys. It must also be remembered that although these are helpful, the cane and other aids do present a barrier between the child and the environment and there must be occasions when a child is encouraged to feel the door, the wall, the cupboard and so on. As with all areas of the curriculum it is a case of using different activities to meet different objectives.

CONCLUSION

It is critical that all adults involved with the child agree with the philosophy that any improvement in independence is worth working for and worth spending the time required on. There is no doubt that all mobility training takes time, which will be all the greater if the children's needs are complex. It is, however, not only the training that has time implications. If the child learns a new skill in a training session, it is, as has been argued elsewhere in this book, vital that this skill is used in daily living activities. For example the new skill that has been achieved may be that the child can now move independently along a corridor. If the class is moving from the classroom to the dining hall along this particular corridor it is essential that the child uses this skill in the real situation.

It is to be hoped that now consideration is being given to the mobility and orientation education for these children and young people, the momentum for providing this will increase and that it will be regarded as the right of every pupil to be assessed in their skills and to receive the appropriate provision for their particular needs.

7

The environment

INTRODUCTION

There are two aspects to the mobility of children with disabilities. The first is clearly the person with the disability and the second is the environment in which the person moves. There is no doubt that people with disabilities are handicapped as much by society and the environment as by their particular disability. An article which highlights this in a forceful way is one by Finkelstein (1991), who suggests that 'disability is a socially caused problem'. He imagines a thousand or more disabled people, all wheelchair users, who have collected together in their own village. Everything in the village is designed for wheelchair users.

> One thing the wheelchair architects quickly discovered was that because everyone was always in wheelchairs, there was no need to have ceilings at 9'6" or door heights at 7'2". These heights could be lowered considerably. A few able-bodied people came to live in the village. Soon all were suffering from dark bruises they carried on their heads. Furthermore, all were suffering from acute backache. Soon a number of reports were produced by social workers, doctors and so on and eventually a number of aids were produced to help the able-bodied. These included toughened helmets to wear at all times to guard against the knocks on the low ceilings and door frames. The able bodied were also given special braces which gave support whilst they moved around in a bent double position. These people were unable to find employment. One who tried to get a job as a television interviewer was told that the village society would find the helmet wearing unacceptable. Charities were organised and the logo consisted of a figure bent double, staring at the ground, carrying a collecting box on its back. One day the able bodied realised that if the buildings in the village were altered, their problems would be solved. However, the wheelchair users felt that this was unacceptable and that such demands simply showed that the able bodied were unable to accept their disability.

This article typifies the attitude of many people and demonstrates how attitudes need to be changed and the extent to which it is the physical environment that causes many of the difficulties of people with special needs.

Many of the modifications to the physical environment which need to be made are small ones, which with knowledge and forethought can be made quite simply and with few financial implications. It is important to realize that many of the changes which will be made to facilitate the access to the environment for disabled people will also improve access for non-disabled people. The adaptations should be more than just the elimination of hazards. Ideally, adaptations should ensure access and positively encourage travel.

There are major problems which need to be overcome if the environment is to be made to meet the needs of people with disabilities. The first of these is that many neighbourhoods and buildings were built long before the full rights of disabled people were recognized, although it can be questioned if rights of access are truly accepted, even today. Many buildings will require huge modifications if they are to be truly accessible. For example, the building in which I am writing has a lift up to all the main floors. Unfortunately, there are also mezzanine floors set between the main floors which all involve a flight of six steps. This is, in fact, a fairly minor example of bad practice in design which occurred over 30 years ago. The financial implications of putting in lifts is quite considerable and the cost of remediating more extensive examples of bad practice can be enormous.

The second problem is that some policy makers are not fully committed to equal opportunity of access for disabled people. There are many organizations for disabled people who have been fighting their cause for many years with, in some cases, little effect. Policy makers will need convincing, by the general public, that it regards commitment to improving access as critical and essential. It will probably take a very long time before the general public can be persuaded to play its full part in supporting people with disabilities and their fight for equal access to the environment.

The third problem is that sometimes the various groups supporting a particular disability disagree about the modifications to access required. An improvement modification for one group may make life more difficult for another. As an erstwhile 'wheelchair pusher' the sight of a ramped kerb lifted my spirits more than somewhat, and in one college in which I worked students in wheelchairs were asking for the increased use of ramped kerbs. They also asked for less use to be made of the textured pavements, some of which were made with fairly high and solid 'bumps' which made wheelchair travel difficult. However, students with visual impairments found the textured areas on pavements very helpful while the ramped kerbs could be dangerous. Students with visual impairments who used a long cane but who also had difficulty walking in a straight line could find themselves walking across the ramped kerb and off into the road. In addition, the siting of ramps is sometimes most inappropriate. They are frequently placed alongside steps without kerbs or protection at the side. This makes them dangerous for people with either physical or visual disabilities. Further consultation between policy makers, town planners, architects and representatives from all the groups of people with disabilities is needed. In schools, equal access for pupils with disabilities will require the full support and co-operation of the staff. In the current situation, where schools are managing their own budgets and financial resources are being discussed, the needs of a small minority of pupils may come very far down on the list of priorities. In order to make school buildings accessible for pupils with physical disabilities, lifts and wheelchair ramps will be needed and toilets may need adapting. These major costs may be borne by the local authority, while other costs may need to be paid for by the school and are essential if children with physical disabilities are to be placed within mainstream schools. As Tingle (1990) says, 'Our aim is to minimise the mismatch between the children's needs and what the school environment is able to offer'.

This chapter does not have the space, and nor is it the place, to describe in detail all the various building modifications that are possible and desirable to improve access for children with disabilities. Advice on the individual situation can be obtained from your local Health and Safety Officer, and a very useful book, *Designing for Pupils with Special Educational Needs* (DfE Building Bulletin 77), was published in 1992. Nevertheless a summary of the principles underlying modifications is given below, as these clearly affect the opportunity for children's mobility and orientation in school and the community.

GENERAL PRINCIPLES FOR IMPROVING THE ENVIRONMENT

The design of school buildings is influenced by a large number of regulations which govern, among others, the safety aspects and also include the principles which should be included in order to make school buildings accessible for children with disabilities. For this to be done appropriately, it is necessary to consider the wide range of individual needs that different children will have.

Children with physical disabilities

Assumptions are often made about the needs of children with disabilities without a real look at their particular strengths and difficulties. For example, there will be children who will be able to climb stairs, but who are unable to walk the long corridors that exist in many of our schools. For these children, it will not be necessary to spend a lot of money putting in stair lifts, but it may be necessary to provide wheelchairs to enable them to travel from classroom to classroom. Another example is the child who has a poor sense of balance or other minor motor difficulties. She or he may be able to negotiate the entire school campus, except for some irregular steps at the front entrance to the school. This child could be helped by renovating or renewing the steps or by providing handrails.

Children with visual impairments

Children with visual impairments can also be helped by adapting the environment. A study made by the Royal Institute of Architects (1981) looked particularly at the needs of people who are visually impaired. This study listed a six-point plan to maximize safety and efficiency in the use of buildings:

1 Simplicity of layout.
2 Good lighting and elimination of glare.
3 Use of colour and tone contrast.
4 Use of texture contrast and tactile clues.
5 Good acoustic condition.
6 Clear, large graphics at eye level.

Organization and layout of classrooms and school buildings

For all children with disabilities, the organization of buildings as a whole and of individual classrooms will do much to facilitate mobility and orientation. A complex school campus will be difficult for children with learning difficulties to understand. Their independent travel may be hindered because they are unable to orientate themselves to the complexity of design. However, it needs to be said that simplicity of layout does not mean 'sameness'. Most people will have had the experience of being in a strange building which consists of corridors and wings which all have the same design and the same decor, and of not being sure which part of the building they are in. Such buildings can easily be made more comprehensible through a sensible use of colour.

The entrances to schools are frequently preceded by steps. It may be possible to provide a ramp to the door of the school. This will be decided by the number and height of the steps and also the space around the entrance. A ramp of quite a steep gradient will certainly help a wheelchair user gain access to the school, but only if someone is there to push the wheelchair. To enable a person in a wheelchair to have independent access, ramps must have a maximum gradient of 1 in 12. This means that for every foot of height there needs to be twelve feet of ramp. This is the maximum gradient allowed and it is still fairly steep. Many people in wheelchairs would find this difficult to negotiate. Because of the space needed for the ramp, these are often sited in a zigzag fashion. Unfortunately, many of these zigzag ramps do not allow sufficient space at each turn for people in wheelchairs to change direction! If the particular location is considered inappropriate for a fixed ramp, there are portable ramps which can be kept within the entrance to the school and moved outside when needed. However, the use of these depends on there being someone available to move them. An adaptation to school entrances which would go some way to helping many pupils with physical disabilities who do not use wheelchairs would be to ensure that there are handrails and that the actual steps are not too steep, through the provision of half steps if necessary.

Once inside the school, there may be many other difficulties to contend with. For many children with motor disabilities, some of the problems can be eased through attention to the type of door handles and the strength of door springs. Fire doors must have strong self-closing springs, but these are difficult to negotiate for children who are using wheelchairs or crutches and also for children who have poor physical strength or who have problems of co-ordination. It should be ensured that doors, wherever possible, are accessible. Children should be able to get through doors without difficulty. Sometimes a door handle of the lever type is easier for the children to use than turning door handles. This is simple and cheap to provide and can really make a difference to some children.

Children with special needs will also require more space to move around. Moving with crutches, a stick, rollator or wheelchair takes more space than moving around without aids. This space can often be provided by looking at the arrangement of furniture within the school. Corridors and entrances to rooms should be made as obstacle-free as possible. Encouraging independence will involve willingness and commitment from everyone in the school building. This willingness is not only shown in the design and layout of the buildings, but also in the care and maintenance taken of any modification that is made; this is discussed later in this chapter.

Another dangerous area within the indoor environment is around flights of stairs, especially the stairwells. Figure 7.1 demonstrates this.

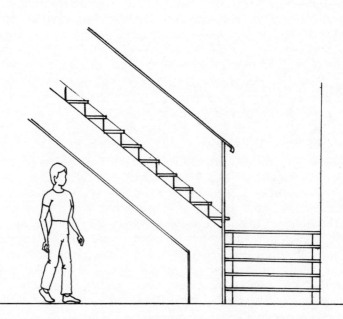

Figure 7.1

The long-cane techniques will not detect these overhanging obstacles. Most young children will walk under these without any problem. However, children grow and many young people are in danger of bad knocks on the face or head through badly designed stairwells. In addition, many schools have free open stairs and these are also dangerous. Pupils will of course be taught where these danger spots are. However, in the hustle and business of daily life, pupils can get disoriented and forget the specific locations of hazards. Stairs and stairwells should be boxed in to prevent anyone walking in from the side or knocking their head on protruding concrete. Colour can also be used to highlight the edges of stairs. This can be very helpful for pupils with low vision; stairs which are all one, possibly drab, colour can tend to look like a ramp rather than a flight of stairs. This modification is quite common in public buildings. Advice is needed before this is done. In one school, a helpful caretaker painted the edges of a flight of stairs with white paint. Unfortunately, the width of the white strip in relation to the gradient of the stairs meant that the flight of stairs still looked like a slope, only this time a white one.

Windows are yet another source of danger. The writer has encountered children who have met with injury through walking into windows which opened outwards to the playground. These children were those who had useful levels of vision but were unable to see the window glass, particularly if the sun was shining through it. Care should be taken to ensure that such windows are not opened on the ground floor. Large expanses of window glass can also be dangerous to fully sighted children as well as visually impaired children. These should be identified by some sort of marking.

Other factors in the design of schools which should be taken into consideration are: the provision of lifts where possible; adaptations of toilets to make them appropriate for the use of children with special needs; and ensuring the width of doorways is adequate for children using wheelchairs. It is also critical to consider the evacuation of children with special needs in the eventuality of a fire. All staff in the school need to know the correct procedures and the appropriate exits for the individual children. The children themselves need to be aware of the procedures and escape routes, so that they can take some of the responsibility and begin to help themselves. Door frames can be highlighted through the use of a contrasting colour, another example of where good practice for visually impaired children will also be good practice for all children. Classrooms need to be organized appropriately to meet the needs of all the pupils. In special schools this is probably easier to do, but even here there needs to be an assessment of the layout to ensure that it provides easy access and encourages independence. The aisles between the desks need to be wide enough for them to be negotiated by the pupils with physical disabilities.

If pupils are to be given the responsibility for their own books and for collecting and returning equipment, it must be made possible for them to do so. The storage space must be examined to see that all the children can access the cupboards and that these are clearly identified for them. Large print or Brailled labels may be necessary.

Two documents which are helpful to schools when considering these issues are available from the Department of Education and Science (now the Department for Education): *Access for Disabled Students to Educational Buildings* (DES, 1984a) and *Designing for Children with Special Educational Needs in the Ordinary Classroom* (DES, 1984b).

Lighting

There is no doubt that improving the illumination of the environment is one of the best ways to improve the environment for children and young people who have low vision. This is generally true, not only for these children but also for the school population as a whole. The important factor to realize and remember when considering this aspect of the environment is that a good level of lighting does not mean simply more of it. It is not necessarily helpful to add additional lighting in order to improve the environment. To understand the difficulties caused by inappropriate lighting think of driving a car and trying to look through a dirty windscreen when the sun is shining directly in your eyes. However, as Best (1992) says:

> Children with different eye defects and levels of vision will have different preferred lighting levels. Some children, notably those with cataracts, may see best in lighting levels which are slightly lower than normal as this causes the iris to open and allows of the lens to be used for vision.

Best goes on to point out that it is not possible to make a direct relationship between eye conditions and the most suitable lighting conditions for pupils. These will vary with the individual pupil and the effect on vision of a particular eye defect. This is clearly another area which requires assessing before embarking on a programme of mobility and orientation.

Appropriate lighting can be helpful in two ways. The first is in the addition of extra lighting in order to do a particular task, such as reading. This is usually referred to as task lighting. The second use of lighting is most applicable to enabling mobility and orientation, and this is environmental or background lighting. There needs to be sufficient levels of appropriate environmental lighting for the pupils to move around safely.

One main source of lighting is the sun. The effects of a bright sun on the mobility of some children with low vision was discussed in Chapter 1. In Britain the levels of light from this source are very variable and it is impossible to know from day to day, even from hour to hour, quite what the level of lighting from the sun is going to be. It is certainly necessary in summer months for children who are averse to bright light to carry sunglasses or a visor with them. At times sunglasses may be needed to be worn indoors, even by children who do not normally wear them. Many modern schools have large window areas, for example along corridors, and the effect of the sun streaming through these can produce glare, which can be very disorientating. Where there is a danger of this situation occurring, on the south side of a school for example, window blinds should be fitted. However, the amount of sun is very variable and if blinds are fitted it has to be the teacher's responsibility to ensure that these are used when necessary – something else for the busy teacher to remember. The other main source of lighting is through electricity: filament light-bulbs or fluorescent tubes. The latter is the preferred type for background lighting. As the light from fluorescent tubes comes from a large area, the illumination of the environment is better than from the normal filament bulb. In addition, there is less likelihood of glare.

School buildings should be looked at and any dark areas examined to see if there is a possibility of adding additional lighting. For some children with low levels of vision, moving from a brightly lit area to a dimly lit one and vice versa can cause great problems. The provision of additional lighting can be very helpful. It is also important to stress that what improves the environment for pupils with restricted vision is also helpful for everyone else and is general good practice.

The main aim of environmental lighting is to provide a sufficient level of illumination to prevent the creation of any hard shadows (Best, 1992). Strong shadow lines, in both the internal and external environments, can often be interpreted as a change in walking level, a step up or down for example. Recommendations for levels of lighting are given in the *Code for Interior Lighting* (Illuminating Engineering Society, 1977).

Decor

Much can be done to make the environment more accessible through consideration of decor. I have already mentioned the dangers of glare for children with visual impairments and much glare can be prevented through the use of non-reflective paint, with a matt rather than a gloss finish. The use of colour has already been mentioned in relation to making the layout of buildings easier to understand and in highlighting particular features, such as handrails and door frames. Colour can also be used to highlight particular routes or specific junctions and landmarks around the school through the use of coloured strips on the floor surfaces. If colour is to be used in this way, there needs to be good contrast between the identification of objects and the background. The identification of routes is perhaps more appropriately used in buildings which are visited by many people with visual impairments, rather than in a school where pupils should be able to learn the routes needed in a short length of time. The needs of pupils with learning difficulties may be helped in this way. In addition to the use of colour to aid orientation, the use of texture contrast should also be considered. It can be helpful if different surface textures are sited at each end of flights of stairs, at entrances and at main intersections in the school.

Maintenance and care of buildings

It is important to remember that as individuals and groups in society there is much we can do to facilitate the ease of access for people with a disability. It is known by safety organizations that thousands of accidents happen within the home, many of these occurring while people are moving around. Any situation which causes an accident to a fully mobile person must necessarily be doubly dangerous to those with mobility problems. (We would all do well to look around our homes on a regular basis and check for danger points, whether or not there is a child or adult with a disability who will be moving within it.) Objects left on the stairs are a danger to everyone, not just to people with disabilities. The objects are often concealed from view. Stairs are an obvious possible source of danger. Worn or badly fitting carpeting or linoleum is well known as being the cause of many trips or falls. Highly polished floors, though attractive, can be dangerous for fully mobile children as well as those who have mobility problems.

The school policy should be that clutter is avoided, particularly in the aisles in the classroom and in the corridors of the school. Pupils and staff should avoid leaving bags, books and clothes on the floor, as these will be dangerous for pupils with special needs. Care must be taken that flexes and cables are not allowed to trail. If this is necessary, then all the pupils should be warned about their presence. Regular maintenance of the buildings must include the painted edges of stairs described earlier. If the paint becomes dingy, scraped or dull, the stairs can become more of a hazard to the pupils with visual impairments than if nothing had been done.

THE OUTDOOR ENVIRONMENT

Individual schools and the members of staff within them may be able to do little to improve the general outdoor environment, except of course within the boundaries of the school. It is necessary, however, to understand the difficulties that can be encountered by children with special needs. Teachers and other members of staff will be supporting the pupils in their mobility and orientation programmes and an understanding of the problems caused by the environment will enable them to support the children effectively. The staff will also be aware of particular hazards and can forewarn the children. It should also mean that more members of the general public will give their support to any suggested improvements.

Pushing a wheelchair or walking under blindfold with a long cane along some of the pavements in this country quickly focuses the attention on cracked and uneven paving stones. Some of these cracks, which before appeared to be minor, soon take on a similarity to deep precipices or tall mountains! The appearance of some smooth asphalt areas becomes a lifeline, resulting in a lessening of physical effort and tension. Major hazards are caused by cars parked on kerbs or bicycles draped around lamp-posts. One carer of a partner in a wheelchair said 'Derek would like to take himself to the shops, they're not far and he would enjoy being out by himself for a bit. But he can't, the cars on the pavements often mean that there's no space on the pavement for him to get past them. I worry about him having to go into the road – a busy shopping street – for him to get past the cars!' A blind traveller, experiencing the same sort of situations, declared cheerfully 'Anything parked on the pavement gets a whack of my cane!'

Similar problems are caused by street furniture such as rubbish bags and shop displays on the pavement. An examination of many of the building works on pavements, such as when laying cables or renewing pipes, will show that these are bounded by the flimsiest of plastic tape, placed several feet above the ground. Visually impaired travellers, using long canes, do not detect this and are in danger of falling and hurting themselves very badly, as many will confirm from bitter experience. The mess left by dogs on pavements is perhaps not so dangerous, but for wheelchair or blind travellers it is extremely unpleasant. Overhanging branches of bushes and trees can be both frightening and dangerous for travellers with visual impairments.

Many of these dangerous and unpleasant hazards are caused by ignorance and thoughtlessness on the part of the general public, shopkeepers and local authorities. There are obvious remedies. As members of the general public, care can be taken to leave the pavements clear of obstacles and to ensure that our own garden does not have trees that overhang the pavement. Local authority workers must provide safeguards when any building work is taking place. Road works and scaffolding should be protected by substantial barriers. Scaffolding posts should be painted in clear contrasting colours and these should be illuminated at night. Local authorities and providers of services, such as British Rail, also have a responsibility to ensure that signs are as visible as possible. Signs and other public notices should be in bright contrasting colours. In addition, care must be taken over the siting of the signs and notices. They should be placed in the optimum position for visibility but not so that they pose a hazard for travellers with special needs. An example of a poor position would be where notices are placed at head level with the danger that people who are visually impaired will bump into them. The same can be applied to wall-mounted telephone boxes, as Figure 7.2 shows.

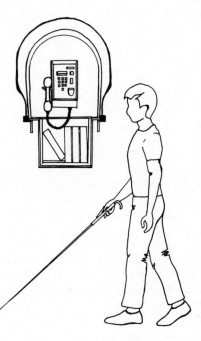

Figure 7.2

Any new road crossings provided by the local authority should be the audible type, and there should be textured approaches, particularly where there are dropped kerbs. The quality of the texture's surface needs to take into consideration the needs of both physically disabled and visually impaired people, that is, detectable enough to be felt under foot or identified through the cane, but not so raised that the texture causes problems for those using crutches or wheelchairs. It is also helpful if textured paving can be provided to show where there is a bus stop. Wardell (1976) reports the use of a pocket device to activate audible crossings. This is not as yet in general use, but would seem to be a development that should be pursued.

Transport

An excellent book (Uslan *et al.*, 1990) on access to travel for visually impaired people gives detailed information on many aspects of travel. Unfortunately, as it is American, many of the practical examples cited, such as the numbering of streets and 'blocks' and various aspects of public transport, are inappropriate for other countries. However, the authors report on one man with a visual impairment and his description of travelling to work, which highlights the efforts needed for all travellers with special needs. He says his journey to work involved taking buses, negotiating subways, using inter-city trains, changing trains and buses, and coping with the general public. Many people with visual impairments say that they are physically and mentally tired before they reach their place of work. At the end of the day, the same effort and concentration has then to be made for the return journey.

One invention that has possibilities is the 'Talking bus stop', known as ELSIE (Electronic Speech Information Equipment). This was devised by Dr Tony Heyes of the Blind Mobility Research Unit at Nottingham University. On pressing a button on the bus stop post, the traveller receives messages such as 'Good morning. The time is 9.45. The buses that stop here are: the 87, next bus due at 10 o'clock; the 89, next bus due at 10.10.' ELSIE can also detect and identify approaching buses through a bus identification unit. This operates through an infra-red light transmitter (although a camera system also has possibilities). As travellers hear the bus approaching they receive information of what number bus is arriving and its destination. This device has so far only been piloted in a small English town. However, this or technology like this will soon become more common, at least in our major cities.

An RNIB survey (1992) showed that 56 per cent of all blind and partially sighted people do not travel beyond their immediate locality. This increases the need for a method of signals which will give the blind and partially sighted traveller information in a way that they can use, and the requirement that the information is provided on time and is relevant (Harris and Whitney, 1994). A Smart Sign is a sign which is triggered and controlled from a distance by the user. A few of its possibilities include warning that a dangerous position is being approached or to tell the traveller where she or he is. Current research into Smart Signs involves looking at technologies that are suitable for transferring information to the user, which will lead to the useful benefit of increased mobility for blind and partially sighted people. The future looks exciting.

The general public

As has been seen, there are many restrictions in the physical environment which impede the mobility and orientation of people with special needs. However, even these can be overcome if the general public is aware of how to be helpful appropriately and is willing to be so. The importance of the help being appropriate is shown by the following comment from a young woman with a visual impairment:

> For example, you get on a subway car and you're fine. All you're carrying is a purse. A pregnant woman with 16 packages insists on getting up and giving you her seat – and she drops all her 16 packages while she's doing it. But she still insists you take her seat. It really can wreck my day and my ability to negotiate safely if I allow myself to feel embarrassed by such incidents.   (Uslan *et al.*, 1990)

This statement agrees with Corn (1989), who talks about challenges that are often created by people unaware of the special needs of others.

The general public, of course, includes school staff, although the in-service training, recommended in Chapter 3, should give all of those working in schools an expertise not available to the general public. Schools can do much to raise the awareness of the general public, as they are visited by a large number of people. The waiting area of the school can display posters and leaflets for people to read, which can be very useful, both to raise general awareness and to give specific advice on guiding people with visual impairments and in helping people with other special needs. Many organizations, such as Scope (formerly the Spastics Society) and the Royal National Institute for the Blind, publish useful material for this purpose.

Much of what is required from the general public is not specific expertise but common sense and an open mind to listening to the views of people with disabilities, such as the one expressed at the beginning of this section. In the school situation, this open-mindedness will lead to solutions such as the pupils having two sets of books, one at school and the other for home, to save the burden of transporting them, or having all the work for the day in one ring file to save carrying a number of books around during the day. Older pupils, such as members of post-16 classes in the secondary school, can often be made responsible for helping pupils with their mobility and orientation.

There is an obvious need for there to be many public education programmes for the general public and specific training courses for personnel in certain service industries. Some of this already exists. However, such training should be available to transport personnel, shop assistants and staff in restaurants. A useful booklet to assist with this is produced by the Partially Sighted Society (see the additional reading list).

This basic training, which should be part of an induction course for new staff, would include acquiring a detailed knowledge of the building or area, with specific safe routes for people with special needs. It should also include opportunities for the staff to understand and practise the principles for giving help in an appropriate way, such as:

- Speak to make contact – gestures may not be seen.
- Introduce yourself and your particular role, speaking clearly without shouting, facing the person in case he or she is a lip reader.
- Offer help and ask precisely what is required. Do not assume that you know what the person's needs and requirements are.
- Give clear verbal instructions.
- When guiding people who are visually impaired, do not hold on to them. Allow them to hold on to your arm.
- When pushing wheelchairs do not go too quickly, as this can be frightening for the users. Try to avoid as many bumps for the traveller as possible.

8

The provision of mobility training

THE HISTORY OF MOBILITY TRAINING

You might think that mobility education, for visually impaired people at least, would be a main feature of their education. This has not been so and it is fascinating to overview the development of mobility education for the blind and visually impaired. Before education for blind people began in Britain, there had always been small pockets of philanthropic provision for blind people. These mainly consisted of the provision of care and some sheltered workshop activities; institutions never saw their role as educating blind people to become independent. It was often left to the individual blind person and their families to find ways of becoming independent. In an article written in 1947, a blind Italian man remembers his early experiences with his father, who clearly had some high objectives for his son. He says 'In the country, he taught me to walk beside him and to recognize by ear, the proximity of a wall, a hedge, or tree'. He added 'If we were crossing a square, he taught me to cross it on the diagonal, explaining that this was the quickest way' (quoted in Bledsoe, 1980).

Bledsoe also reports on a blind Englishman, John Metcalf, who was a road builder and travelled about on foot and on horseback, once guiding a sighted individual through a bog on a dark night. Bledsoe describes an old print of Metcalf which shows him holding a cane so long that it reached almost up to his hat. Without any formal training, both these people's skills were clearly excellent, but very few achieved this sort of independence.

Early developments in the United States of America

An early example of formal training in mobility and orientation in the United States of America began as a result of the efforts of Dr Samuel Howe, and was developed by one of his teachers, Francis Campbell. Campbell, himself blind, initiated a programme of physical education and almost certainly included in his physical training of the pupils some orientation and mobility. Campbell himself used a moderately long cane. He later came to England and founded the Royal Normal College, now the Royal National College at Hereford.

Long-cane training was developed at the end of the Second World War by Dr Richard Hoover, who was working with soldiers who had been blinded in the war. He recognized that what was needed most by these veterans was to be able to move around independently. Hoover, who was an army sergeant at the time, disregarded the short wooden canes that had been used by blind people for centuries, and developed a systematic method of travel for the blind soldiers employing a long, light, functional cane made of lightweight aluminium. After the war, this method of cane travel was taken over and refined at the Veterans' Administration Hospital in Illinois (Bledsoe, 1980).

Learning the technique devised by Hoover, and known as 'foot travel', gave the veterans the opportunity to move safely, efficiently and independently in a variety of locations from the relatively safe indoor areas to the downtown areas of large cities. The veterans developed self-confidence by learning to use special techniques and skills, and by using their remaining senses to the full in order to pick up information from the world around them. Very few advances are made without dissension, and training in the use of the long cane was no exception. There was an outcry from many blind people who felt that the use of a cane was degrading, identified them as blind, and was in any case totally unnecessary. However, the long-cane technique gradually became accepted by blind people and by those who worked with them. Eventually, the first official mobility and orientation instructors were trained and established at the Hines Hospital, but these instructors worked only with war veterans. It was not until 1960 that Boston College received a government grant to begin courses for mobility and orientation instructors for other blind people.

There was still no mobility and orientation education in schools. As Bledsoe (1980) points out, the majority of blind children were educated in special schools in a controlled and secure environment, and such training was not thought to be important. In addition, in the early part of the nineteenth century, the traffic problem was virtually non-existent. It was felt that an optional and *ad hoc* use of a cane was sufficient.

Guide dogs

The use of guide dogs appears to have begun in Germany after the First World War, and was a development which followed from the use of dogs for military purposes. Training dogs for use by blind people was started by a trainer of search dogs for the army and there are reports of over 4,000 dogs being in use in the 1920s. In the United States of America, Dorothy Eustis established the Seeing Eye association in 1929. There was a certain amount of opposition to the use of guide dogs, but despite this, the movement grew.

Provision of guide dogs in Britain

In 1931 the first guide dogs were trained in Britain, but it wasn't until 1943 that the Guide Dogs Association was established. The first training centre opened at Leamington Spa. In 1994 there were approximately ten main training and other satellite centres, which service guide-dog owners throughout Britain. There are approximately 4,000 trained guide dogs in Britain with approximately 700 being trained each year. These are given to newly blind clients and also to previous owners whose dogs have grown too old to be able to work. In recent years the age restriction has been reduced to 16 and eligibility is dependent on reports from social services, mobility officers and medical personnel. The medical reports not only contain the necessary information on the visual condition and prognosis of the prospective owner, but also a statement that he or she is fit enough to own and use a guide dog. A visit is made to the home of the blind person, to see that the facilities are suitable for a dog, and as Brooks (1989) reports, 'help can be given with improvement to fencing for the garden and so on, if needed'. Once the blind person has been accepted, it is necessary for them to undergo a period of intensive training and this is usually done on a residential basis. Training will include how to take care of the dog generally, how to control it and how to interpret the dog's signals. There is a very careful support service and each owner is encouraged to report in at regular intervals in order that they can receive advice regarding 'their mobility or their dog's health and welfare' (Brooks, 1989).

Development of mobility training in Great Britain

In the late 1950s and 1960s, communication between both blind people and workers for blind people in America and Britain led to the first centres for training mobility and orientation specialists. However, in Britain there was some controversy surrounding the work of these specialists and the training given to clients still focused on training young, fit, adventitiously blinded men in the long-cane technique. Mobility officers were employed only by social services departments or by charitable organizations. Gradually, the needs of elderly blind people for mobility training began to be recognized. This was important, as by far the largest proportion of visually impaired people are over 70 years of age. The students on the training courses did not receive any guidance on a mobility curriculum for children. It was still not regarded as necessary for children to receive any formal training and, even if they did require it, it was assumed that the same curriculum used with adults would be suitable for children. Special schools for blind people varied very much in their philosophy towards independent travel, some encouraging their pupils to move as freely as possible and others not doing so.

However, in the last 20 years or so, pressure from schools, colleges and visually impaired people themselves resulted in provision being made available to meet the needs of children. In the late 1960s, Leonard (1967) argued forcibly that mobility should be taught to children and included in the special school curriculum. He said 'Although we may say to ourselves, "Little Betsy is walking quite well", we may have to admit that Little Betsy is walking about as freely as an arthritic old lady on a set of cobble stones, that her shins are frequently bruised and her nose not infrequently scratched. We should not accept this as good enough.' He also added 'in the fullness of time, it is not unreasonable to hope for the employment of teachers with special qualifications in teaching mobility'. Tooze, a teacher in a special school for blind children, undertook training to teach mobility. She recognized that the needs of children who were congenitally visually impaired were very different from adults who had lost their sight later in life. In 1981, she produced her book *Independence Training for Children and Young People* and also produced a video on children's mobility called *Stepping Out*.

In Britain in the late 1970s and early 1980s, special schools for visually impaired children began to employ mobility specialists. These specialists varied very much in the way they worked. Some felt it was not appropriate for children under twelve years of age to receive any formal training, whereas others wanted to become involved with the children as early as possible. In addition, training was usually given only to pupils who were considered as blind. The needs of partially sighted children for mobility and orientation programmes have only recently been recognized and are even now not fully accepted. Although there have always been pupils with visual impairments within mainstream schools, and the number of these has increased very greatly over the past 20 years, the mobility needs of these pupils have largely been neglected. Very few of these pupils received any formal mobility education. Advisory services which support pupils with visual impairments began to argue for mobility input for these children, and this began to be developed in a number of regions of the country during the mid-1980s.

THE CURRENT SITUATION

The majority of mobility specialists still operate within social services departments in local authorities. They mainly work with elderly blind people and, because their caseloads are large, are often unable to give much help to children in schools. All special schools and colleges now employ mobility teachers, most of whom will have received special training to teach children. These specialists are employed either as full-time members of the school staff, or as part-time or visiting specialists. They may be teachers or non-teaching staff who have been seconded to undergo a training course in mobility, or mobility specialists who have opted to work with children. Mobility and orientation skills are recognized by the special schools as being a critical part of the total curriculum for children with visual impairments. Even so, there can still be a gap in provision for children who attend residential schools. While the majority of pupils with visual impairments receive excellent training during the school terms, it is sometimes difficult for the school to provide this training during their holidays in their home locality. This has two important implications. First, any skills learnt during term-time may be forgotten during the holidays, particularly the long summer holiday. The second implication is even more critical. The lack of training during holidays may mean that the pupils become efficient at travelling in the locality of their school but have no independent travel in their home area.

There are about 20 local education authority educational support services for visually impaired people who have mobility specialists as part of their team, which is just under 20 per cent of all services. Some services are able to call on the mobility officers from social services departments, and some mobility posts are jointly funded by social services and education departments. The majority of teachers within education support services for visually impaired children are fully aware of the importance of mobility programmes, but several of them have stated that they have difficulty in convincing their employers of the critical nature of this input. Many mobility specialists do not feel confident in teaching children and young people with multiple disabilities and many of these children's needs remain unmet. Some teachers who have undertaken a qualifying course to teach visually impaired children are able to teach basic mobility. In most cases, however, their teaching caseloads are so large that they are not able to spare the time to give the regular sessions which are needed for mobility programmes.

Accessing mobility programmes

The 1981 Education Act requires statements of special educational need to be made for children whose needs cannot be met within the mainstream school. These statements are legal documents which should include details of the pupil's strengths and difficulties, the strategies needed to provide access to the full curriculum, and any special curriculum required for the individual pupil. The special curriculum would include a programme of mobility for those children who need it. An assessment of children's need for mobility and orientation education should be made as part of the procedure for collecting information for the statement, and as part of the final statement there should be a clear indication of the children's need for a programme of mobility. The assessment procedure should include information from a qualified teacher of visually impaired children, in which case there will be the expertise available to make an argument for the provision of mobility training. Unfortunately, even when this is done there are too many occasions when the mobility needs of the children are not met. This is partly because of the financial implications of providing mobility teaching on a one-to-one basis. It can also be due to the shortage of mobility specialists for children, or even the administrative difficulty of arranging for social services staff to work within schools. It also has to be said that part of the reason for the failure to meet these special needs of children is a lack of understanding and commitment from policy makers and administrators.

If it is doubtful whether the statementing procedure ensures the provision of mobility education for those pupils with statements, the danger of not meeting the needs of pupils without statements is likely to be great. There is a large number of children and young people with severe visual impairments who are not statemented. Walters (1994) comments that there are 'diverse rates of statementing between different authorities' and that these rates vary from 0.8 to 3.8 per cent of the school populations. Stone (1990) found that only a third of the children with visual impairments who were supported by LEA advisory services were the subject of statements. This leaves many pupils in mainstream schools in a very vulnerable situation. There should also be encouragement for the development of whole-school policies on mobility and orientation.

The 1988 Education Reform Act

There are, at the time of writing, concerns as to how the 1988 Education Reform Act will affect the education of pupils with special educational needs in mainstream schools generally. For a minority group, such as visually impaired children, the effects of the new arrangements for the local management of schools may be traumatic. While it is still hoped that support services for sensory disabilities will be retained centrally by the local education authority, the emphasis on resource-led support may mean that the provision of mobility training becomes even more difficult. Certainly for the children without statements it is unlikely that 'schools will buy in all the appropriate and available LEA provision' (Walters, 1994). In addition, Walters states that the level of provision of in-service training for special educational needs is currently very low. All these factors together mean that the future indeed looks bleak. It appears that this is true not only of pupils in mainstream education but also of those in special schools as well. Several headteachers of special schools for visually impaired children have said that they wonder about the future provision of such specialist expertise. If these concerns are valid, and they appear to be, the possibility of extending and expanding services to meet the needs of all children with low vision and children with multiple disabilities, let alone to children with other special needs, seems unlikely. Parents, headteachers, school staff and advisory services face an uphill struggle to ensure that children and young people's needs in this area are met in the future.

Fortunately, professionals are aware of this and are arguing for quality of provision. Two documents have recently been produced by and on behalf of educators of visually impaired children. The first is *Guidelines for Maintaining the Educational Entitlement of Pupils Who Are Visually Impaired*, produced in 1994 by a group of specialist teachers of children and young people with visual impairments. They state as one of the major entitlements for these children 'mobility and orientation appropriate to the need of ambulant or non ambulant blind and partially sighted pupils of all ages, from diagnosis'. They also state this as one of the major entitlements for 'pupils who have complex needs in addition to visual impairment'. The second document is *Draft Guidelines for Consideration by Those Bodies Responsible for the Provision of a High Quality Educational Service for Blind Children*. Tobin and Pitchers, leading experts in the field of visual impairment, were commissioned by the Royal London Society for the Blind 'to produce these draft guidelines as a contribution to the debate on what should constitute a quality educational service for blind children' (1994). In this document the authors discuss quality assurance and development. Mobility and orientation is one of the aspects that is included and it is hoped that both these documents will unite the educators in the field of visual impairment in the struggle to ensure that children's needs are met.

Parents

Parents and immediate carers are the people who will have the most influence on the movement and mobility of their children. The very first motivation for the child to move will be, or be provided by, them. They will be the ones to argue for the input of a mobility specialist or a teacher who has had mobility experience. But although the input and guidance from such a professional will be very helpful, the parents themselves have the most to offer. They will know their child best, his or her likes and dislikes, and preferred toys. It is their voices, hugs and smiles which will be the best rewards for the child. Once the child is crawling and then walking, parents can do much of the teaching. By following the child's curiosity and that of any siblings, as well as their own sense of fun and adventure, the parents can 'become very good orientation teachers' (Webster, 1980). The suggestions made in Chapter 2 were made as much with parents as with professionals in mind.

When the child reaches school, parents may feel that their child needs more formal mobility and orientation programmes and it is their right to ask that these be provided. It may be quite hard to make such a request and requires some determination on their part. If their child has the protection of a statement then the assessment and review procedure will give the parents the opportunity to request such intervention. The parents may need even more tenacity if their child has not been through the statementing procedures.

The role of the mobility specialist

The role of the mobility specialist who works with children and young people is a varied one and this will be particularly true of the specialists who work within the mainstream situation. Not only will they be working with a variety of children and young people, differing in age and ability, but there will also be a variety of educational establishments in which to work. This is part of the enjoyment of supporting children in the mainstream situation. It does, however, make the role a different one from that of mobility specialists who work within special schools. Although the programmes that are implemented within special and mainstream schools will be very similar, there will be different and perhaps additional stresses on mobility specialists working with pupils who are integrated. A few of these stresses are described later in this section. The various functions of mobility specialists include: supporting parents, working with colleagues from other professions, assessment, devising and implementing programmes, and providing awareness and in-service training sessions. Some of these have been referred to throughout this book, others are described here.

Working with parents

One major role of the mobility teacher is to work very closely with parents. There is no possibility of overstating the importance of parents in the lives of their children. Parents' support for the mobility programme throughout the child's life will be crucial. They will need to understand the general aims of the mobility programme and to be kept informed of the specific objectives at each stage. The mobility specialists will need to understand the parents and their feelings and reactions to the idea of mobility training, and these will differ for each individual parent. Many specialists are not able to work within the home situation with children of pre-school age, but some, although by no means all, qualified teachers of visually impaired children will also have studied mobility as part of their training course. These teachers will be able to provide support for the parents and implement early mobility and orientation education and will appreciate contact with any other mobility specialists in the locality. It is also important that parents are informed of the programmes initiated in school and of their child's progress in order to provide continued support at home.

Assessment

Assessment, as has been discussed throughout this book, is a continual process. Each mobility lesson is an assessment situation and the teacher needs to be alert throughout in order to observe the child carefully. The sameness of practising a route with a pupil time after time can sometimes lead to the teacher missing subtle changes in the pupil's behaviour which give useful pointers for new approaches which could be used. The pupil may react differently to a teaching situation than she or he did during the previous lesson, and the teacher needs to be careful not to miss this. Any such information must be given to the other staff in the school who will be able to reciprocate and therefore further the assessment process.

Self-evaluation

It is essential that mobility teachers are professional in their own self-evaluation. Working with a succession of pupils throughout the day may leave little time for this, but a few moments must be taken to do so. The mobility teaching situation does have the danger that each lesson is not always taught to the highest standards. Children arriving late for lessons, adverse weather conditions and the routine of many lessons may lead to the occasional lackadaisical approach. It is worth mobility teachers asking themselves the following questions at the end of every lesson:

- Did I really prepare for that lesson? Had I set a specific objective for it? Was this achieved?
- Did I use the lesson time effectively?
- Did the pupil get tired or frustrated? Was he or she sufficiently challenged? Did he or she enjoy the lesson?
- What feedback did the pupil give me through conversation, gestures or in other ways?
- Could I have used a different strategy? A new route? A new route can re-motivate both teacher and pupil.
- Was I always alert to the safety aspects of the lesson?
- How could my presentation of materials or teaching approaches have been improved?

Confidentiality

The one-to-one teaching situation which mobility demands, and the trust of the pupil in the teacher which has to be a part of the working relationship, often lead to the pupil confiding in the mobility teacher on many personal issues. This may lead to a difficulty with confidentiality and the mobility teacher must be quite clear on his or her own policy regarding this. What information does need to be communicated to others? How will this be explained to the pupil? Which confidences can be kept between the pupil and teacher?

Inter-professional communication

Rehabilitation workers in a local authority social services department appreciate the need for communication and co-operation with other colleagues. In the same way, mobility specialists working within schools must appreciate that they have no ownership to their expertise – it is for sharing. Mobility specialists cannot be effective in their role without the co-operation of teachers and other staff in the schools. Effective inter-professional working should be, and in the majority of cases is, current practice in special schools for visually impaired children, but even here there are occasions when different professionals protect their own area of knowledge. It may need a period of building relationships to break down these barriers and mobility specialists must do all they can to ensure that they are not guilty of any defensiveness. It does not help the pupils.

Much of the communication that takes place between the mobility specialist and colleagues from other disciplines will be made through written reports and these need to be of a high standard. Reports should not include a lot of terminology which will not be understood by the recipients. Reports should be clear and concise, describe progress to date and set realistic short- and long-term objectives and give precise details of the programme which will be initiated. They should also include suggestions on ways in which the programme can be supported and developed by others.

Attitudes

Mobility teachers working within the mainstream situation may have on occasions a difficult path to tread. Their expertise may not be recognized, accepted or wanted by many mainstream staff. The latter may well see specialists as people who just 'take the children out for a walk' and it will require tact and diplomacy on the part of the mobility specialist to deal with such attitudes without alienating the staff in the process. An equable nature is essential. There will be days when specialists arrive late to a school because of traffic jams or delays at the previous school or home. This late arrival can sometimes produce comments such as 'Been shopping again?'. On other days it is possible to arrive at school to be greeted with the cheerful comment 'Sorry, forgot to tell you, Jamie's not here today'. The only response is a 'gritted teeth' smile and 'Oh, that's all right, don't worry'.

Professional support and development

Mobility specialists in any work situation can sometimes feel isolated. They may be the only person in an area who is in this role with its particular problems and difficulties. It is worth building a personal professional support system and there are several ways of doing this. VIEW (Visual Impairment: Education and Welfare) is an association of professionals, parents and carers of children and adults with visual impairments. Within the association, there is a Chapter for rehabilitation workers and mobility specialists, which runs conferences and establishes networks. An association of Mobility Teachers in Special Education (MISE) has also recently been formed. The teachers meet three or four times a year to support each other and to develop curriculum documents on mobility for children. Both these associations can provide helpful support.

There are many current studies and research projects which have implications for the mobility education of children with special educational needs. It is important that mobility teachers keep up to date with these studies which will feed into their teaching. They should also ask for second-level training which will enable them to develop further the skills they need for the various parts of their role, such as working with other professionals, changing attitudes and in-service training.

The training of mobility teachers

Until a few years ago, there were two types of training course that were available for people who wanted to work within the rehabilitation services, that is, services for adults. One of these courses trained mobility officers and the other was for technical officers. Technical officers supported and helped people who were blind in their own homes, providing them with specific aids and teaching them such independent living skills as cooking, housecraft and so on. Both these professionals received a six-month training course, half of which was spent on a practical placement. There were three centres for such training, two run by Regional Associations for the Blind, one in Leeds and the other in London. The third centre was in Birmingham and came under the aegis of the Royal National Institute for the Blind. A few years ago it was recognized that there was a good deal of overlap between the roles of the mobility officer and that of the technical officer. The two courses were combined and then became a year-long course and the new professional worker was called a rehabilitation officer. The courses are a blend of theory and practice and include a study of the causes and implications of a visual impairment, the implications for people with an additional hearing loss, and deal with any aspects of learning and teaching. Developing counselling skills is seen as an important part of the courses. As the majority of the students will be working with the adults in the community, all of the issues surrounding the care of adults within the community are discussed. As part of their training, students must learn how to travel wearing a blindfold, and they are taught by another instructor in the teaching situation as though they were blind. They learn how to do blindfolded what they are going to teach. One director of a college programme has said that this helps to develop the habit of thinking like a blind person when it comes to analysing the travel situation. Similar activities are undertaken wearing spectacles which simulate visual difficulties. From this they learn to teach people with visual impairments to conquer various travel problems.

The courses were supported by the Department of Health, which gave a grant to the training agencies. A Training Board was established to monitor the quality of training within each centre. The Guide Dogs for the Blind Association, recognizing that their clients also needed the services of rehabilitation officers as well as the guide dog services which they provided, also set up a training course. A further development was the alignment of some of the training courses with institutions of higher education. This meant that students on the courses could obtain an academic award as well as the professional training course and this was welcomed by many of the professionals in the field. Unfortunately, the awards were varied, including certificates, diplomas and masters-level degrees, and this has led to further confusion among workers in the field and employers alike. Currently, the whole issue of training is under review as the Department of Health has withdrawn its grant to these agencies which train mobility specialists and two centres have had to close. In addition, the National Training Board which reviewed all training courses and worked to ensure a parity of standard has also ceased to exist. This is likely to have an adverse effect on the training of mobility specialists, first because the opportunities for training are now limited, certainly in terms of the geographical location of centres, and second, there is a danger that there will be a fragmentation of training. In times of financial restraint, it may be tempting for employers and others to opt for the cheapest course available, which may not be the one that will produce the most qualified professionals. The people to suffer from these changes will, of course, be the children and adults with visual impairments.

Several of the training centres also run short courses for people who want to teach mobility to children, in which there is far more emphasis on the developmental aspects of the education in mobility and orientation. These courses vary in length, content and style of delivery and those wishing to follow a course of training should investigate the various courses to see which one will meet their training needs. Here again, while some training agencies will continue to strive for excellence, there is the danger that short, cheap courses will emerge and prove attractive to employers who are funding students and to students themselves.

Parents, providers of mobility education and young people themselves will first need to argue for the provision of resources to fund specialist personnel, and, second, try to ensure that those personnel who serve the children do have the high level of expertise that the children need and deserve.

CONCLUSION

Leonard, one of the early instigators of mobility education for visually impaired children, said 'Look at the children in your care now and look at a group of sighted children of the same age. And if you are not satisfied with the comparison, you can be assured that there is a lot which can be done here and now to narrow the gap' (1969).

The writer strongly believes that the same is true for all children with special educational needs and that parents and educators must demand that this gap is narrowed. Teachers supporting children with visual impairments in schools for children with learning difficulties have said that they are now being asked to extend their mobility teaching to other pupils in the school. The schools themselves are beginning to be aware of the needs of other pupils for mobility education. It is to be hoped that current educational policies and legislation will not prevent further developments in this area.

9

Case studies

The following case studies are of children and young people with whom parents, the writer and other colleagues have worked. The studies are included so that parents, teachers and carers may first understand the kind of input that may be given by a mobility specialist at various times of the pupils' lives, and, second, because the programmes which are described in the studies may be helpful to readers in their own involvement with children with special needs. The studies do not follow the same format as they were compiled by different people, and all the names have been changed.

NEEMA

Neema, 2 years old, was congenitally blind and had no useful residual vision. There were no other identified physical or health problems. She lived with both parents and there was other family support close by. The parents, particularly her mother, spent a lot of time caring and playing with her. When the mobility specialist was first asked to see Neema at the age of 2 she had recently begun to walk. At the instigation of the health visitor, Neema and her mother had just started to attend a mother and toddler group.

First visit

On the first visit, Neema was found sitting on a large rug, surrounded by toys which were mostly soft toys, that is teddy bears and rag dolls. There seemed few other toys, apart from a rattle and a small ball. Neema didn't appear to reach out for any of the toys. Her parents tended to pass toys to her and place them in her hands. Neema's parents appeared to instigate all of her play and Neema really only fiddled with what she was given. According to her mother, Neema's language was well developed for her age and she was able to make herself understood regarding meal times and toileting. However, during the visit the only words Neema used were to do with her toys, such as 'ball' and 'dolly'. However, despite this, Neema appeared to be quite an alert and cheerful little girl.

Neema's ability to walk freely around her home environment appeared very limited. She only demonstrated any movement towards the end of the session and this at the direct instruction from her parents. Once up on her feet, she moved towards her mother's calling and clapping, but at no time did she make contact with anything about her. Neema had a few mannerisms which became apparent when she began to walk. When she stopped walking, she rocked from side to side and also poked her eyes. Neema's parents were extremely concerned about these, which was the main reason why contact was initially made through the health visitor to the mobility specialist. Her mother also remarked that they had been very much against any outside intervention and had only recently agreed to any assistance. The health visitor had instigated the attendance at the mother and toddler group. Her mother had found that Neema enjoyed the group and was beginning to interact with the other children.

On this initial visit, the main observation was Neema's reluctance to interact with her environment and to initiate any movement.

After discussion with the parents, the following list of objectives was proposed:

1 *To introduce Neema to a route which was related to her current activities.* This was to be the route to her toy box to fetch a toy and then to her rug. The armchair and the coffee table were to be part of the 'route'. The aim was to make Neema more aware of the environment around her. Neema should also be encouraged to select the toys with which she wanted to play.

2 *To develop a more appropriate selection of toys and play items.* A visit to a toy library was suggested, so that a toy could be played with prior to purchasing it, to assess whether it would be of use and appropriate to Neema's needs.

   Neema should be introduced to a wide variety of toys, such as those with sounds or music, or which are different in texture, shape, weight and size. This would help Neema begin to build up a repertoire of concepts and develop the use of her hands. A further suggestion was to find Neema toys and activities which have a 'cause and effect' factor, so that she has to make an action to get the resulting sound or other effect.

3 *To develop spatial and movement concepts.* The parents were asked to help Neema to develop such concepts as up, down, left, right, under, over, below, on top of, inside, and so on. This can be done

through activity songs and rhymes, through physical play, and through her parents describing her movements.

4 *To help Neema to initiate her own movement.* The parents would encourage this through physical and verbal prompts. Neema should spend more time outside and be encouraged to explore the garden. It was also suggested to the parents that they should take Neema for walks along the road (rather than always in the pushchair, as had happened until then).

5 *The parents would try and enlist the support of other close family members,* such as the grandparents, in an effort to expand Neema's experiences.

6 *The parents were encouraged to keep a diary of Neema's progress* and to note the activities which she seemed to enjoy most.

7 *The mobility specialist would visit on a fortnightly basis* to work with Neema and monitor her progress. The specialist would also visit the parent and toddler group with Neema and her mother for a few sessions.

SCOTT

Eye condition: Congenital cataracts (hereditary) and nystagmus.
Acuity: 3/60 in both eyes.

Scott was 5 years old and an only child. His father commuted daily into London, returning home late in the evening, leaving Scott's mother to carry most of the worry and responsibility for him. Scott had surgery when he was 2 years old to disperse the cataracts in both eyes. This left him aphakic (the eyes could no longer accommodate because of the removal of the lenses). Scott wore contact lenses and bifocal spectacles. Unfortunately, he had suffered from infections in his eyes since the operations and had been having regular check-ups to prevent further damage to his eyes. Scott's referral to the mobility specialist came from the authority's Education Advisory Service. Scott's mobility was excellent in the home and garden, but he was very frightened when moving around elsewhere. His mother was clearly worried about letting Scott move even in the garden without her staying very close. Scott was due to start school after the summer holidays, which began a few weeks later.

On the initial visit Scott was observed moving around his home and garden. He appeared confident and relaxed in his familiar surroundings and had good posture. Scott was able to use his limited residual vision to locate brightly coloured toys and objects.

Scott appeared to have a fairly limited use of language, and was generally quiet. During discussions with Scott's mother it became apparent that she was very worried about how Scott would cope in the school environment – he had not been to nursery school because he used to cry if she left him. He had spent very little time away from his mother. His mother was worried about how he would find his way around, and said that he became clingy and frightened in strange environments. She had low expectations of his future and had never met any other parents of children with visual impairments. The name of a local support group was given to her and she seemed interested.

I suggested a number of games and lent Mrs Williams some books and leaflets which included ideas for developing Scott's body and spatial awareness. The games included hunting for hidden objects in the garden. It was hoped that the activities would also help develop his confidence and self-concept. I explained to Scott's mother about the importance of encouraging him to explore every-day objects around the home to help him develop an understanding of his environment and to give real meaning to his language. I also explained the need for her to give verbal descriptions when they walk along the road. We also discussed the need to develop Scott's auditory skills by listening to different sounds within the home, and by making use of listening tapes and stories.

On a second visit, I observed Scott with his mother on a short walk outside and with her help did an informal low-vision assessment. I explained how she could make the walk more interesting for Scott by letting him explore the surroundings on the way and by giving an incentive at the end such as the local sweet shop! On the walk we helped him begin to develop an appreciation of the environment by showing him lamp-posts, bus shelters, trees and street furniture; to build up his understanding that pedestrians are on the pavement and cars in the road, and to introduce a basic understanding of road safety by having him listen to the different types of engine sounds: cars, buses, motor bikes, etc.

A further objective was to encourage Scott to think about tactile clues and gradients, to develop his auditory skills by encouraging him to listen to sounds around him: music playing, birds singing, a dog barking, a pushchair passing him. Scott should be taken out in different weather conditions to observe the difference in sound and to feel the wind and rain on his face. Obviously the above experiences will need to be introduced gradually as Scott is not confident away from the home environment. However, I thought it was important that Scott's mother was given lots of ideas to try, and these were all things that she could work on while out with him.

As Scott tended to walk very close to his mother and she often had an arm around him, I suggested she held his hand or encouraged him to hold on just above her wrist so that he gets used to walking sensibly and in a guiding position, which might be useful when Scott starts school. We also went to a park as Scott enjoys the swings (a good incentive), and which is an area where we could encourage movement, exploration, co-ordination, the use of his residual vision, and generally increase his confidence moving around. I would continue reinforcing and extending the above skills during my visits as Scott, I hoped, came to trust me.

The immediate objectives were as follows:

1 To start an informal but structured mobility programme at home, working on the suggestions stated above.
2 To make contact with the local education authority to arrange mobility lessons when Scott started school.
3 To make contact with the school to arrange for Scott, his mother and myself to visit the school before the summer holidays. I would try and make arrangements for Scott and me to visit the school several times during the summer holidays.
4 To arrange an awareness programme for the staff at the school.
5 To keep in close contact with the Education Advisory Service.

Extract from report written two months later:

1 Scott is going to be supported by a visiting peripatetic teacher for visually impaired children, who will be giving support particularly in literacy and numeracy – timetabled – using a resource room in the school.
2 Discussed Scott's mobility problems and the implication of these within the school environment, with the peripatetic teacher.
3 Arranged a meeting with the headteacher and classroom teacher. Scott is the first visually impaired child to attend the school. The classroom teacher is very worried about how Scott will cope, and the adaptations she will need to make to accommodate him. Toured the school with the headteacher and classroom teacher and looked at areas that could be difficult for Scott.
4 Advice given on safety issues and areas that could be improved such as colour contrast, lighting improvements or reduction of glare, use of textures, painting a strip on the steps, tactile indication at the top of steps, and clear, bold colour-contrasted signs. Fortunately the staff were receptive to these suggestions and appreciated that the improvements would benefit all the children and would increase their awareness.
5 I explained to the headteacher that I would be spending time during the holidays familiarizing Scott with the layout of the class-

room. With the headteacher, I looked at the routes that Scott would need and identified specific landmarks. Suggested that tactile clues are put on Scott's desk, coat peg, and locker to give him confirmation when he has located them. After further discussion with the headteacher and in answer to some of her questions the following points were noted:

a Scott may be tentative in exploring and delayed in the development of some of his motor skills.
b Although Scott may become confident in familiar surroundings, when on school visits or while swimming he will need verbal descriptions and reassurance that an adult is watching close by him.
c It is important that Scott takes a full part in all physical activities or games to increase his body and spatial awareness and his stamina.
d Scott has some mannerisms when he walks (he tends to flap his hands when excited and jumps up and down). I have found that by just touching Scott on the arm he will stop flapping. This would be suggested to the rest of the staff.

Mobility in the school

During the summer holidays I took Scott and his mother to the school to familiarize him on the most important routes:

1 Familiarization of his classroom, the position of his desk and the use of specific landmarks.
2 Routes to the toilets, cloakroom, dining room and the playground area. As Scott has a favourite dinosaur toy I used this to make the lessons fun and enjoyable for Scott and asked him to show his 'teddy' the way around his new school.
3 Scott and I made two visits to the school without his mother. He appears to trust me, is not as clingy as he is with his mother, and walked for part of the time by himself. This was, of course, while the school was empty and Scott may react differently when there are a lot of children around. I intend to be at school for his first morning and hope to talk to his class teacher beforehand.

INSET training for staff

I have liaised with the peripatetic teacher to put together a training day for the staff, which we will cover jointly. The programme will include:

1 Scott's eye condition, prognosis and implications regarding his low vision.

2 Practical experience using simulating spectacles.
3 General awareness training, such as using Scott's name at the beginning of a sentence so he knows he is being spoken to.
4 Stressing the importance of all the staff in the school, including kitchen and playground helpers, knowing about Scott's visual problems.
5 Discussion of routes learnt.

Continued programme

I will continue to liaise with the peripatetic teacher and classroom teacher, working with them and giving support/advice on mobility matters when required. I will include Scott's mother in his mobility programme; she is already feeling less fearful and I am making a video to show Scott's progress over the months.

I wish I had spent more time with Scott in the playground rather than in the school buildings as it is large areas of space which seem to frighten him; this was perhaps a mistake on my part. I should also have given the father the opportunity to be included in the mobility programme.

PETER

This report is taken from a parent's account of a programme which they initiated.

Peter is 30 years old and has severe learning difficulties. He has always had a strong independent streak and has tried to copy all that his elder brothers do.

Peter attended a school for children with severe learning difficulties up to the age of 16. He got to school by taxi which was provided by the local education authority. When he was 11 we wondered if he could manage the journey by bus. The bus left from the bus station, which was about six or seven minutes' walk away. There were two roads to cross, but one was governed by a pelican crossing and the other by a zebra crossing. The bus journey to the school took about 20 minutes and Peter would have to learn to get off the bus about four stops before the end of the bus route. After that, all he had to do was walk round the corner to the school. We spent one summer holiday making the bus journey about three times a week. We practised crossing the roads and finding the right bus in the station. Peter had the bus number written down on a piece of paper and he had to find it. It was really a case of finding the right section of the station. After we had made the trip several times, we gave Peter the exact money, so that he could practise giving it to the driver. This was the bit that worried him most. He had little language and hated using it with strangers.

After a few weeks, one of his brothers took him to the bus station, took him to the right bus and saw him on it. I followed behind the bus with my car; he knew I was there. I saw him get off at the right stop and walk round the corner to school. Then Peter made the journey to the bus station by himself, while one of us followed some yards behind, and again I followed him in the car. I felt confident he could do the whole thing by himself and one day he did it, with me still following in the car. He always had his name, address and destination on him, just in case.

I rang up the transport place at Shire Hall and cancelled the taxi. They wouldn't let me do it and said Peter had to go in the taxi. We were furious. It took us a whole term to get our way. Once we did, Peter travelled every day by bus and back again. There was one drastic day, when the school rang me up and said he hadn't arrived. I flew to the bus station to look for him, but no sign. I got the car and did all the route to school. Still no sign. I informed the police and went back to the bus station. Then Peter arrived off a bus. He had got on a bus with the right number, but it was going in the opposite direction. (I found out later that it had stopped at an unusual place in the bus station because of some road works.) The driver said he had taken Peter's money as he got on, but at the end of the bus route had realized he was still there. Peter showed him his 'information card' and the bus driver told him to stay on the bus all the way back. I asked Peter whether he was frightened – he said 'No' and I'm not sure whether that's a good thing or not.

KERRY

Background

Kerry, 11 years old and totally blind. Both eyes removed when she was 4 years old as a result of complications following a bad fall and resultant injuries. Fully sighted up until then. No other disabilities; normal, healthy, able child.

Lives with her mother and younger sister in a fairly quiet market town. Older brother lives with father, following parents' divorce. Both siblings are sighted and very supportive and accepting of their sister's impairment. Kerry is very familiar with the town centre and uses her cane very well there. At present she attends the local primary school, which is all ground level and open plan. The school caters for about 200 children, and Kerry is the only visually impaired child attending. Due to commence at the local secondary school next term, where she will again be the only visually impaired child; the school already has two or three children who are physically disabled.

Present mobility

All pre-cane skills; trailing, body protection techniques, etc., to a very high standard. Very confident long-cane user, excellent orientation skills and sensory perception. Consistently accurate route memories. Very confident around present school and home area. Mother takes Kerry out quite often on a tandem bike around the countryside. Kerry is also a very keen swimmer. At her present school she is allowed to integrate fully with her peers at break and lunch times without any extra adult supervision. No problems or worries ever caused by this.

Presenting problems

1 New school layout is very different: three storeys, much bigger and busier, about 800 children.
2 New routes for Kerry in and around school buildings and playground. Will have to learn to identify classrooms, etc.
3 Upset at moving to new school and fact that not all her current peer group will be transferring with her.
4 Lack of teachers' experience in dealing with a visually impaired child.
5 Danger points in school – cupboard edges, stairwell, doors, etc.
6 Attitude of headteacher towards Kerry being allowed to move around school and playground unsupervised by an adult.
7 Possibility of situation arising whereby one or two of Kerry's peers become 'responsible' for her while in school.
8 Adolescence – Kerry may refuse to use her cane for fear of being too conspicuous in her new surroundings.

Programme

1 Take Kerry into the school during the holidays to have 'dry runs' of her main routes: registration class, toilets, dining hall, recreation area, etc., using trailing and/or long cane safely and appropriately, appreciating that she will have to be aware that the corridors will be very busy at various times.
2 Make a safety check of the school with the local authority agent in order to identify hazards requiring attention, such as padding head-height cupboard and shelf edges, blocking off or lining open

stairwells, tactile strip at top of flights, rounding off bench corners, 'uniforming' corridor doors, etc.
3 Put forward an awareness training package for staff, also an up-to-date report on what Kerry can do, to try to prevent staff and other pupils doing more for her than necessary.
4 Diplomatic assertion to staff of the value and relevance of mobility training, and of Kerry's right to it.
5 Encourage liaison between all parties and parents, hopefully to foster better connections, so that any mobility work I do will be reinforced between lessons both at home and in school.
6 Arrange formal observation sessions with the headteacher, to show just what Kerry is capable of, or perhaps video her on a particularly busy and difficult town route to show that she can move around safely in a potentially hazardous situation without the need for adult intervention, pointing out that the physically disabled children in the school have poorer balance than Kerry, and are therefore potentially in greater danger of being knocked down than she is. I would also point out the possible damage to Kerry's self-image and confidence if the headteacher insists on constant supervision, regardless of the fact that neither Kerry nor her parents wish this, and that I as a mobility specialist deem it to be inappropriate.
7 Keep parents informed of progress and proposed future input as often as necessary.

Conclusion

It is vital for Kerry's settling-in period at her new school to be as worry free as possible, and this should be the priority of everyone concerned with her. Given her exceptionally high standard of independent mobility there is no real reason to regard her as any more of a physical risk to herself or other pupils than any other normal child on the brink of adolescence, with the usual degree of self-obsession and rebellion. At a time when she will be attempting to fit in with a new peer group any singling out could be very detrimental to what will be a fairly fragile ego for the next few years, and this aspect of her development of self-belief will have to be recognized by staff and parents alike.

BENJAMIN

Age: 10 years.
Visual impairment: Anophthalmia.
Other handicaps: Physical disabilities and severe learning
difficulties.

Mobility history

Benjamin spends the majority of the time being pushed around in a wheelchair. He can stand and support his own weight through holding on to a rail and so on. He can also walk with an adult holding one hand or by holding on to a rollator with wheels which is guided by an adult. When sitting on the floor, Benjamin does not attempt to move out of his own body space. However, when he is sitting in a low chair Benjamin will shuffle down to the floor and sit cross-legged.

Mobility programme

To make use of the little independent movement that Benjamin had, it was decided that he should be encouraged to shuffle down the stairs on his way to the classroom each morning.

Benjamin and the mobility teacher will walk to the top of the stairs and sit down on the top step. To begin with, Benjamin will be moved physically down each step, placing his hands either side of his body for support. As Benjamin begins to understand the movement and to initiate it, the physical contact and guidance will be reduced.

Progress: one year later

After about a year of this programme, Benjamin did move slowly one step at a time, with a member of staff still sitting next to him on the stairs. He did this independently, though with a great deal of verbal encouragement. Benjamin, once he had reached the bottom of the stairs, continued on his way to class with a rollator.

Next stage of the programme

As Benjamin would eventually be moving to senior school it was thought appropriate to teach him next how to walk down the stairs. He will be encouraged to go down sideways and to keep both hands on the rail. He will be shown how to place his feet correctly.

Current achievement

Over a period of months Benjamin has progressed quite well. He is still not completely independent but he uses the stairs up and down and this has encouraged his parents to try this method at home now Benjamin is more confident.

JENNIE

Age: 9 years.
Vision: Some sight in lower field of right eye.
Other handicaps: Left hemiplegia.

Mobility history

Jennie arrived at school two years ago and was always very insecure in her movements. Although she could walk, she preferred to shuffle on her bottom across the floor. She was taught to trail walls, but did this in a crab-like movement with both hands. When faced with crossing a space, Jennie would either walk all the way around the walls or revert to her shuffling movement.

Programme

It was decided to introduce Jennie to using a walking stick. This was to be held in her right hand as a means of support. The long-term aim was that she might progress to using a long cane.

Progress

Jennie took to using the walking stick fairly easily. She began very gradually to learn to move independently.

One day, when Jennie was sitting outside, she picked up a large, strong twig from the ground and began walking with it. The mobility teacher made a collection of different sorts of twigs. Over a period of weeks, the walking stick was forgotten and Jennie was allowed to choose which twig she used. She continued to move around quite happily, minimally using the twig for support. The teacher showed Jennie how to find the grass and paving with the twig through the sound.

The mobility teacher introduced Jennie to a symbol cane, explaining that it was a special twig. The symbol cane was chosen because it was light and fairly flexible. Jennie accepted this, but gave the cane some fairly rough treatment. A long cane was introduced but

Jennie did not like this as much. She was asked only to walk down a corridor with it before transferring either to the symbol cane or one of the twigs.

Jennie's resistance to the long cane is not as strong as it was and it is hoped that this will continue to decrease. The use of the symbol cane or twig is not satisfactory as Jennie's posture is not good when she is using them. She is able to discriminate between different ground surfaces and to detect obstacles, but she cannot yet detect drops. Trying to get Jennie to accept the long cane will continue as part of the total orientation and mobility programme.

HELEN

Helen, aged 16, was born blind. She is to leave school this term and move on to the further education college. This report summarizes her mobility history and her training and achievements.

Her mother and father allowed Helen to explore when she was very young and she was allowed to travel and play in the house, garden, and neighbourhood in her early years. This was a rural area and she was mostly accompanied by her sister.

Helen attended a special school for visually impaired children and her formal mobility training began when she was 11 years old. After one year of training, Helen had learnt to use the long cane efficiently. She uses a cane which is slightly long for her, which gives approximately four feet of stopping distance. Helen is happy to be seen with the cane as she feels it is a symbol of her independence.

The following is an account of one of her routes:

Helen leaves the school and turns left out of the school gate. The first hazard is a wide school entrance. While crossing this, Helen follows a gravel shoreline on her right side with the cane to keep from veering into the street. Helen listens to every car that passes in the road and judges the distance of the cars in order to keep the correct distance. Having passed the school entrance, she turns and crosses the road using an audible crossing point and continues along the road. Helen looks confident and says she knows she is still on the correct route. A car in the parallel street has just gone by and it is about the correct distance away from Helen on the left. Interpreting the sounds of parallel and cross traffic and being able to align her body with them are very important orientation skills for Helen (Webster, 1980).

Helen continues walking with confidence, keeping the cane in as much contact with the ground as possible. As the cane tip makes contact with grass to the right of her, she pauses and recognizes that she has veered away from the pavement into a driveway.

Helen begins to anticipate Elm Road, which should be coming up soon. She prepares to find the drop at the kerb and does so. The junction of Elm Road and the main road is a busy one. Helen listens for a few seconds to the traffic flow and judges when it is safe to cross.

This is a short example of the mental processes that Helen uses along one section of the route. Helen and her mobility instructor have spent many hours practising the different methods and techniques of crossing at various types of road junctions. The rest of Helen's route includes crossing four more streets each slightly different, entering Woolworth's Department Store, asking for assistance to locate the sweet section, making a purchase, then returning to school, remembering to reverse all the turns and look for different landmarks.

The high degree of skills that Helen demonstrates may seem impossible to the parent of a young blind child, or it might be thought that Helen was a particularly able young woman. This was not so; many pupils achieve the same levels of independent travel. For Helen, the route was a simple one, a route that she could travel with little concentration and effort. Helen knows the location of all the shops in the local shopping area, and is aware of the traffic controls and traffic flows at each junction. Helen can safely judge when to cross the busiest of streets. At traffic-light crossings, she will ask for help if she needs it. With new road crossings that she has not met before, Helen has the ability to stand at the junction and, by listening to the traffic flow, recognize the type of crossing and the traffic control device in operation.

Helen has learnt to make maximum use of her remaining senses. She has the ability to achieve independent travel through the use of the long cane. With further practice and training, she could travel in any large city. Much of the credit for Helen being able to learn how to travel so well must be given to her parents and the experiences they allowed her to have in the pre-school years.

Additional reading

Books may be borrowed from:
Royal National Institute for the Blind reference library
206 Great Portland Street
London W1N 6AA

Books and leaflets may be purchased from:
RNIB
National Education Services
190 Kensal Road
London W10 5BT

Vision Aid
Guy Salmon House
22A Chorley New Road
Bolton BL1 4AP
(Vision Aid also loans books)

The following may be helpful:
The World in Our Hands, a series of videos and booklets
Games for All of Us
Getting Off the Ground
How to Thrive, Not Just Survive
Move with Me
Get a Wiggle On
Move It!
An Orientation and Mobility Primer for Families and Young Children
Pathways to Independence
The Body-Image of Blind Children
The Comprehending Hand

The Partially Sighted Society is another source of useful material.

Other useful texts include:
Aitken, S. and Buultjens, M. *Vision for Doing: Assessing Functional Vision of Learners Who Are Multihandicapped.* Moray House Publications.

Russell, P. (1989) *The Motor Impaired Child*. Souvenir Press.
Working with Visually Impaired Children (1994). Mobility Specialists in
    Special Education.

Useful journals include:
British Journal of Special Education
British Journal of Visual Impairment (a pack of selected articles on
    mobility and orientation can be obtained from the journal)
Talking Sense
Special Children

References

Bentzen (1980) In Welsh and Blasch, op. cit.

Best, A. B. (1992) *Teaching Children with Visual Impairments*. Milton Keynes: Open University.

Bigelow, A. (1991) Spatial mapping of familiar locations in blind children. *Journal of Visual Impairment and Blindness* **85** (3), 113–17.

Blades, M. (1991) 'The development of the abilities required to understand spatial representations'. In Mark, D. and Frank, A. (eds) *Cognitive and Linguistic Aspects of Geographic Space*. Dordrecht: Kluwer Academic Press.

Bledsoe, C. Warren (1980). 'Originators of orientation and mobility training'. In Welsh and Blasch, op. cit.

Bosbach, S. R. (1988) Precare mobility devices: short report. *Journal of Visual Impairment and Blindness* **82** (8) (October), 338-9.

Bower, T. G. R. (1977) Blind babies see with their ears. *New Scientist* **74** (1057) (23 June), 712–14.

Brooks, M. (1989) In Foundation IMC, op. cit.

Corn, A. (1989) 'Mobility for children with low vision'. In Foundation IMC, op. cit.

Cratty, B. J. (1971) *Movement and Spatial Awareness in Blind Youth*. Springfield, IL: Charles C. Thomas.

Cratty, B. and Sams, T. A. (1968) *The Body Image of Blind Children*. New York: American Foundation for the Blind.

Department for Education (1992) *Designing for Pupils with Special Educational Needs* (DfE Bulletin 77). London: HMSO.

Farmer, L. W. (1980) 'Mobility devices'. In Welsh and Blasch, op. cit.

Ferrell, K. A. (1979) Orientation and mobility for pre-school children: what we have and what we need. *Journal of Visual Impairment and Blindness* **73**, 147–50.

Finkelstein, V. and Brechin, A. (1991) 'To deny or not to deny disability'. In Liddiard, P. and Swain, J. (eds) *Handicap in a Social World*. London: Hodder & Stoughton/Open University.

Foundation IMC (1989). Proceedings of Mobility Conference. The Netherlands.

Fraiberg, S. (1977) *Insights from the Blind*. Horizon Publishing Co.

Garry, R. J. and Ascarelli, A. (1969) Teaching of topographical orientation and spatial orientation to congenitally blind children. *Journal of Education* **143** (2), 1–48.

Gee, K., Harrell, R. and Rosenberg, R. (1987) 'Teaching orientation and mobility skills within and across natural opportunities for travel: a model designed for learners with multiple severe disabilities'. In Goetz, L., Guess, D. and Strewel-Campbell, L. (eds) *Innovative Program Design for Individuals with Sensory Impairments*. Baltimore: Paul H. Brookes.

Gibbs (1994) 'The use of the Hoople'. Unpublished project module. School of Education, University of Birmingham.

Hapeman, L. (1967) Development concepts of blind children between the ages of 3 and 6 as they relate to orientation and mobility. *The International Journal for the Education of the Blind*, 41–7.

Harley, R. K., Merbler, J. B. and Wood, T. A. (1981) *Peabody Mobility Assessment Kit*. Chicago: Stoelting Co.

Harley, R. K., Merbler, J. B. and Wood, T. A. (1987) Orientation and mobility for the blind multiply handicapped young child. *Journal of Visual Impairment and Blindness* **81** (8) (October), 377–81.

Harris, D. and Whitney, G. (1994) 'Smart Signs': using technology to guide the way. *New Beacon* 922, 4–7.

Hart, V. (1980) 'Environmental orientation and human mobility'. In Welsh and Blasch, op. cit.

Hill, E. (1986) 'Mobility and orientation'. In Scholl, G. (ed.) *Foundations of Education for Blind and Visually Handicapped Children and Youth*. New York: American Foundation for the Blind.

Hill, E. W. (1971) *Performance Test of Selected Positional Concepts*. Chicago: Stoelting Co.

Hill, E. and Blasch, B. (1980) 'Concept development'. In Welsh and Blasch, op. cit.

Hill, E. and Conder, P. (1976) *Orientation and Mobility Techniques*. New York: American Foundation for the Blind.

Hill, E. W., Dodson-Burk, B. and Taylor, C. R. (1992) The development and evaluation of an orientation and mobility screening for pre-school children with visual impairments. *Review* **XXIII** (4).

Hill, E. W., Rosen, S., Correa, V. E. and Langley, M. B. (1984). Pre-school orientation and mobility: an expanded definition. *Education of the Visually Handicapped* **XVI** (2) (Summer), 152–61.

Hinton (1988) *British Journal of Visual Impairment* **6** (1), 11.

Illuminating Engineering Society (1977) *Code for Interior Lighting*. London: Illuminating Engineering Society.

Jacobson, W. H. (1993) *The Art and Science of Teaching Orientation and Mobility to Persons with Visual Impairments*. New York: American Foundation for the Blind.

Joffee, E. and Rikhe, C. H. (1991) Orientation and mobility for students with severe visual and multiple impairments: a new perspective. *Journal of Visual Impairment and Blindness* (May), 211–16.

Jose, R. (1983) *Understanding Low Vision*. New York: American Foundation for the Blind.

Kephart, J., Kephart, C. and Schwartz, G. (1974) A journey into the world of a blind child. *Exceptional Children* **40** (6) (March), 421–7.

Koestler, F. A. (1976) *The Unseen Minority*. New York: American Foundation for the Blind.

Law, B. (1987) *About RNIB's Copying Service for Raised Diagrams*. London: RNIB.

Leonard, J. A. (1967) Mobility as a school subject. *Teacher of the Blind* **55** (4), 102–4.

Lessard, K. (1989) 'Mobility for the multihandicapped pupil'. In Foundation IMC, op. cit.

Lord, F. F. (1969) Development of scales for the measurement of orientation and mobility of young blind children. *Exceptional Children* (October), 77–81.

Lowenfeld, B. (1971) *Our Blind Children*. Springfield, IL: Charles C. Thomas.

Lowenfeld, B. (1974) *The Visually Handicapped Child in School*. London: Constable.

McInnes, J. M. and Treffrey, J. A. (1982) *Deaf-Blind Infants and Children: A Developmental Guide*. Milton Keynes: Open University.

Mackey, S. (1988) Teaching mobility to people with Usher syndrome. *Talking Sense* **34** (2) (Summer), 18.

McLarty, M. (1993) Soap opera or bubble tube. *Eye Contact* **7**, 11–12.

Morsley, K., Spencer, C. and Baybutt, K. (1991a). Is there any relationship between a child's body image and spatial skills? *British Journal of Visual Impairment* **9** (2) (July), 41–3.

Morsley, K., Spencer, C. and Baybutt, K. (1991b) Two techniques for encouraging movement and exploration in the visually impaired child. *British Journal of Visual Impairment* **9** (3) (November), 75–8.

Murdoch, H. (1989). Donald steps toward mobility. *Talking Sense* **35** (1) (Spring).

Nielson, L. (1979) *The Comprehending Hand*. Copenhagen: National Board of Social Welfare.

North West Support Services for the Visually Impaired (1994) *Guidelines for Maintaining the Educational Entitlement of Pupils Who Are Visually Impaired*.

Orr, R. (1993) Life beyond the room. *Eye Contact* **6**, 25–6.

Parkes, D. (1989) 'The Nomad system'. In Tatham, A. F. and Dodds, A. G. (eds) *Proceedings of the Second International Symposium on Maps and Graphics for Visually Handicapped People*. London: King's College.

Penton, J. (1991) 'Building study, RNIB Vocational College, Loughborough'. In *Access by Design* (Jan–April), ch. 54.

Pogrund, R. L., Fazzi, D. and Lampert, J. (eds) (1992) *Early Focus: Working with Young Blind and Visually Impaired Children and Their Families*. New York: American Foundation for the Blind.

Raffle, B. (1990) Getting around to it – mobility and children in the mainstream. *New Beacon* **74** (874) (March), 4–5.

Rogow, Sally M. (1988) *Helping the Visually Impaired Child with Developmental Problems*. New York and London: Teachers College Press, Columbia University.

Royal National Institute for the Blind (n.d.) *Mobility Ideas*. London: RNIB.

Shirley, J. (1988) Rob and the soft room. *Talking Sense* **34** (2).

Skellenger, A. C. and Hill, E. W. (1991) Current practices and considerations regarding long cane instruction with pre-school children. *Journal of Visual Impairment and Blindness* **85** (3), 101–4.

Sonsksen, P. M., Levitt, S. and Kitsinger, M. (1984) Identification of constraints on motor development in young disabled children. *Child Care, Health and Development* 273–86.

Spencer, C., Morsley, K., Ungar, S., Pike, E. and Blades, M. (1977) *Developing the Blind Child's Cognition of the Environment: The Role of Direct and Map Given Experience.* Association of American Geographers.

Stone, J. M. (1991) Advisory services – a national provision? *British Journal of Visual Impairment* (Autumn), 92–4.

Stone, J. M. (1992) *Mobility for the Additionally Handicapped.* Birmingham, UK: Distance Learning Unit, University of Birmingham.

Stone, J. M. (1993) 'Transitions'. Keynote response, ICEVH quinquennial conference, Bangkok.

Stone, J. M. and McCall, S. (1990) *Mobility and Orientation* (Unit 15). Birmingham, UK: School of Education, University of Birmingham.

Suterko, S. (1972) 'Practical problems of orientation and mobility'. In Hardy, R. and Cull, J. (eds) *Social and Rehabilitation Services for the Blind.* Springfield, IL: Charles C. Thomas.

Swallow, R. M. and Huebner, K. M. (eds) (1987) *How to Thrive, Not Just Survive.* New York: American Foundation for the Blind.

Thomas, M. (1985) Making sense of the first steps. *Talking Sense* **31** (2) (Summer), 7–8.

Thomas, M. (1987) 'I like to walk with you but'. *Talking Sense* **33** (1) (Spring), 4–5.

Tingle, M. (1990) *The Motor Impaired Child.* Windsor: NFER-Nelson.

Tobin, M. J. (1979) *A Longitudinal Study of Blind and Partially Sighted Children in Special Schools in England and Wales.* Birmingham, UK: Research Centre for the Visually Handicapped, University of Birmingham.

Tobin, M. J. and Pitchers, B. J. (1994) *Draft Guidelines for Consideration by Those Bodies Responsible for the Provision of a High Quality Educational Service for the Blind.*

Tooze, D. (1981) *Independence Training for Children and Young People.* London: Croom Helm.

Ungar, S., Blades, M. and Spencer, C. (1993) Role of tactile map in mobility training. *British Journal of Visual Impairment* (July).

Uslan, M., Peck, A., Wiener, W. and Stern, A. (1990) *Access to Mass Transit for Blind and Visually Impaired Travellers.* New York: American Foundation for the Blind.

Voight, B. (1989) 'A blind wheelchair user speaks'. In Foundation IMC, op. cit.

Walker, E., Tobin, M . and McKennell, A. (1992) *Blind and Partially Sighted Children in Britain: The RNIB Survey*, vol. 2, London: HMSO.

Walker, S. (1992) *Getting off the Ground.* London: Royal National Institute for the Blind.

Walters, B. (1994) *Management for Special Needs.* London: Cassell.

Wardell, K. T. (1976) Parental assistance in orientation and mobility instruction. *Journal of Visual Impairment and Blindness* **70** (8).

Wardell, K. T. (1980) 'Environmental considerations'. In Welsh and Blasch, op. cit.

Webster, R. (1977) *The Road to Freedom.* Jacksonville, IL: Katon Publications.

Webster, R. (1980) *A Parents' Guide to Prepare the Blind Child to Travel Independently*. Jacksonville, IL: Katon Publications.

Welsh, R. (1980) 'Additional handicaps'. In Welsh and Blasch, op. cit.

Welsh, R. and Blasch, B. (1980) *Foundations of Mobility and Orientation*. New York: American Foundation for the Blind.

Willoughby, D. M. (1979) *A Resource Guide for Parents and Educators of Blind Children*. Baltimore: National Federation for the Blind.

—Appendix 1
Body image checklist

(Cratty and Sams)

Name_____ Date of birth _____

Date_____

I   Body planes

1   Identification of body planes

(a) Touch the top of your head ☐
(b) Touch the bottom of your foot ☐
(c) Touch the side of your body ☐
(d) Touch the front of your body ☐
(e) Touch the back of your body ☐

2   Body planes in relation to external surfaces
(horizontal: subject lying on mat; vertical: subject standing)

(a) Lie down on the mat so the side of your body
touches the mat ☐
(b) Now move so your back is touching the mat ☐
(c) Move so your front is touching the mat ☐
(d) Stand so the side of your body touches this wall ☐
(e) Move so your back is touching the wall ☐

3   Objects in relation to body planes
(subject seated with box)

(a) Place the box so it touches your side ☐
(b) Place the box so it touches your front ☐
(c) Place the box so it touches your back ☐
(d) Place it so it touches the top of your head ☐
(e) Place it so it touches the bottom of your foot ☐

II Body parts

4 Body part identification

(a) Tap your arm ☐ (b) Tap your hand ☐
(c) Tap your leg ☐ (d) Tap your elbow ☐
(e) Tap your knee ☐

5 Parts of the face

(a) Tap your ear ☐ (b) Tap your nose ☐
(c) Tap your mouth ☐ (d) Tap your eye ☐
(e) Tap your cheek ☐

6 Parts of the limbs

(a) Tap your wrist ☐ (b) Tap your thigh ☐
(c) Tap your forearm ☐ (d) Tap your upper arm ☐
(e) Tap your shoulder ☐

7 Parts of the hand

(a) Hold up your thumb ☐
(b) Hold up your first (pointing) finger ☐
(c) Hold up your little finger ☐
(d) Hold up your middle finger ☐
(e) Hold up your third (ring) finger ☐

III Body movement

8 Trunk movement
(subject standing)

(a) Bend your body slowly away from me... stop ☐
(b) Bend your body slowly forwards towards me... stop ☐
(c) Bend your body slowly to one side... stop ☐
(d) Bend your knees and slowly squat down... stop ☐
(e) Rise up on your toes... stop ☐

9 Gross movements in relation to body planes

(a) Walk forwards towards me... stop ☐
(b) Walk backwards away from me... stop ☐
(c) Jump in the air... stop ☐
(d) Move towards me by stepping sideways... stop ☐
(e) Move away from me by stepping sideways... stop ☐

10 **Limb movements**
(a–b: subject standing; c–e: subject lying on back)

(a) Bend one arm at the elbow ☐
(b) Lift one arm high in the air ☐
(c) Bend one knee ☐
(d) Bend one arm ☐
(e) Stretch both arms high in the air ☐

IV **Laterality**

11 **Laterality of body** (simple directions, seated)

(a) Tap your right knee ☐
(b) Tap your left arm ☐
(c) Tap your left leg ☐
(d) Bend over slowly and tap your right foot ☐
(e) Tap your left ear ☐

12 **Laterality in relation to objects**
(subject seated with box)

(a) Place the box so it touches your right side ☐
(b) Place the box so it touches your right knee ☐
(c) Hold the box in your left hand ☐
(d) Place the box so it touches your right foot ☐
(e) Pass the box to me with your right hand ☐

13 **Laterality of body** (complex directions, seated)

(a) With your left hand tap your right knee ☐
(b) With your right hand tap your left knee ☐
(c) With your left hand tap your right ear ☐
(d) With your right hand tap your left elbow ☐
(e) With your left hand tap your right wrist ☐

V **Directionality**

14 **Directionality in other people**
(child standing; tester seated facing child. The child's hands are placed on the tester's body parts)

(a) Tap my left shoulder ☐
(b) Tap my left hand ☐
(c) Tap my right side ☐
(d) Tap my right ear ☐
(e) Tap the left side of my neck ☐

15 The left and right of objects
(child seated with a box)

(a) Touch the right side of the box ☐
(b) Touch the left side of the box ☐
(c) With your left hand touch the right side of the box ☐
(d) With your right hand touch the left side of the box ☐ .
(e) With your left hand touch the left side of the box ☐

16 Laterality of other's movements
(child standing)

(a) (tester seated facing child. The child's hands are placed on the tester's shoulders)
Am I bending to my right or left? (Bend right) ☐
(b) Am I bending to my right or left? (Bend left) ☐
(c) (tester seated with back to the child. The child's hands are placed on the tester's shoulders)
Am I bending to my right or left? (Bend left) ☐
(d) Am I bending to my right or left? (Bend right) ☐
(e) (tester stands facing the child; child stands still) ☐
Am I moving right or left? (Move left) ☐

Scoring of the Cratty and Sams screening tests

Scoring is on pass/fail basis. In addition, if a child points to a body part, or makes some response other than that requested, this should be noted.

After each response, care must be taken not to reinforce the response. Thus, after each response, the tester should use the phrase 'Thank you' instead of 'All right' or 'good', which might give an indication to the child.

—Appendix 2
Motor scale

(Harley *et al.*, 1987, p. 378)

Behaviours included in the mobility scales

I Motor scale
  1 Rolls from side to back.
  2 Rolls from back to side.
  3 Rolls from stomach to back.
  4 Rolls from back to stomach.
  5 Rolls from back to sitting position.
  6 Rolls from stomach to sitting.
  7 Rolls from supported sitting to stomach.
  8 Rolls from supported sitting to back.
  9 Maintains sitting posture.
  10 Moves from stomach to hands and knees.
  11 Creeps forward on hands and knees.
  12 Moves from hands and knees to kneeling.
  13 Moves from hands and knees to sitting.
  14 Moves to standing from kneeling
  15 Maintains balance in standing and turning to reach for an object.

II Sensory scale: movement and touch

  1 Reacts to and tolerates touch.
  2 Reacts to and tolerates movement.
  3 Holds object in hand.
  4 Seeks out object after it touches child.
  5 Reaches towards toy.
  6 Reaches for and grasps toy.
  7 Localizes point of touch on body.
  8 Pats and/or tactually explores objects.
  9 Explores container.
  10 Fingers hole in pegboard.

11 Places block in formboard.
12 Locates last hole and inserts peg.
13 Places circle and square in formboard.
14 Places blocks in reversed formboard.
15 Distinguishes two indoor surfaces.

III Sensory scale: awareness and localization of sound

1 Reacts to sound.
2 Makes a grasping motion in response to sound.
3 Turns towards sound.
4 Reaches hand towards a sound-making toy after grasping the toy.
5 Reaches towards a sound-making toy after touching the toy.
6 Reaches hand towards sound-making toy after hearing the toy.
7 Reaches hand towards sound-making toy placed directly in front of the child.
8 Grasps sound-making toy placed in front or to either side of the child.
9 Moves towards source of sound.
10 Moves towards, locates, and grasps sound source.

IV Cognition

1 Orients to two sounds.
2 Takes hand or toy to mouth.
3 Searches for object when removed from grasp.
4 Swipes at or hits suspended toy.
5 Holds one object in each hand.
6 Pats or feels object contacted.
7 Searches for dropped object.
8 Reaches around barrier to get toy.
9 Drops one object to obtain third.
10 Removes toy from small box with lid.
11 Recognizes the reversal of an object.
12 Places block in container.
13 Demonstrates functional use of object.
14 Pulls string horizontally to secure toy.
15 Matches three pairs of common objects (two cups, two shoes, two dolls).
16 Places six to eight blocks in container.
17 Removes small object from narrow-necked bottle.
18 Identifies three common objects.
19 Points to basic body parts.

—Appendix 3

Peabody mobility kit for low vision students

(Motor Skills Cat. no. 33750, pp. 14–15; Stelting Co., 1350 S. Kostner Avenue, Chicago, IL 60623, USA)

Descending stairway

Procedure

Take the student to a stairway which has at least five steps and a banister. Follow the directions given in each step. Precede the student when descending the steps to catch him or her if he or she falls. If the student does not respond to the command in any step, physical prompts may be used to complete the task once. Then return to starting position and repeat the command.

Steps

1 **Place** the student standing or sitting on the fifth step of a stairway.
   Say 'Go down the steps'.
   Observe: The student descends the stairs on his or her buttocks with scooting movements.

2 **Place** the student standing on the fifth step of a stairway, supporting the student under the armpits.
   Say 'Go down the steps'.
   Observe: The student makes stairs-descending movements with his or her legs and feet with support from another person.

3 **Place** the student standing on the fifth step of a stairway.
   Say 'Go down the steps'.
   Observe: The student descends the steps one step at a time placing **both feet** on each step.

4 **Place** the student standing on the fifth step of a stairway.
   Say 'Go down the steps'.
   Observe: The student descends the steps alternating his or her forward foot placing **one foot** per step.

5 **Place** the student approximately three feet from the top step of a
stairway.
Say 'Go down the steps'.
Observe: The student locates the top step, descends the stairs,
and stops on the landing.

—Appendix 4—
Mobility and orientation checklist

Name: Date:

Eye condition: Lessons per week:

                               Type of cane used:

                               Pre-cane skills:

Body orientation	Cratty and Sams test:	☐	☐
Body protection	upper	☐	☐
	lower	☐	☐
	bending	☐	☐
	dropped objects	☐	☐
	search methods	☐	☐
Independent travel	trailing	☐	☐
	square off	☐	☐
	direction taking	☐	☐
	free walking	☐	☐
	room familiarization	☐	☐
School orientation	routes to:		
	classrooms	☐	☐
	toilets	☐	☐
	gym	☐	☐
	hall	☐	☐
	soft play area	☐	☐
	front hall	☐	☐
	dining rooms	☐	☐
	group rooms	☐	☐
	bedrooms	☐	☐

	infant school area	☐	☐
	junior school area	☐	☐
	senior school area	☐	☐
	library	☐	☐
	telephone room	☐	☐
Sighted guide skills	establishing contact	☐	☐
	normal position and grip	☐	☐
	narrow spaces	☐	☐
	about-turns	☐	☐
	switch	☐	☐
	battering ram	☐	☐
	doorways	☐	☐
	ascending stairs	☐	☐
	descending stairs	☐	☐
	sitting down	☐	☐
	table	☐	☐
	cinema	☐	☐
	cars	☐	☐
	speed	☐	☐
	cane and sighted guide	☐	☐
	cane and seating	☐	☐
Symbol cane techniques	indoor cane use	☐	☐
	campus cane use	☐	☐
	outdoor travel	☐	☐
	route memorization	☐	☐
	crossing road	☐	☐
	steps	☐	☐
	pelican crossing	☐	☐
	residential area	☐	☐
	quiet shopping area	☐	☐
	local shops (pass)	☐	☐
	busy shopping areas	☐	☐
	town travel	☐	☐
	bus travel	☐	☐
	train travel	☐	☐
	lifts	☐	☐
	revolving doors	☐	☐
Touch technique	grip	☐	☐
	arm position	☐	☐
	arc	☐	☐
	step (walking in)	☐	☐
	veering	☐	☐

	obstacles (in path)	☐	☐
	ascending stairs	☐	☐
	descending stairs	☐	☐
	doorways	☐	☐
	indoor routes	☐	☐
Outdoor travel	campus travel	☐	☐
	block routes	☐	☐
	road crossing	☐	☐
	use of hearing	☐	☐
	use of traffic sounds	☐	☐
	down kerbs	☐	☐
	up kerbs	☐	☐
	indenting	☐	☐
	outdenting	☐	☐
	route memorization	☐	☐
	quiet shopping area	☐	☐
	local shops (mobility pass)	☐	☐
	busy shopping area	☐	☐
	pelican crossing	☐	☐
	bus travel	☐	☐
	town travel	☐	☐
	train travel	☐	☐
	revolving doors	☐	☐
	escalators	☐	☐
	lifts	☐	☐
Orientation	use of maps	☐	☐
	use of tape maps	☐	☐

Index